The
LEADER
&
The
COACH

Praise for *The Leader and the Coach*

"In *The Leader and The Coach* you get two distinct voices from two unique authors. While those two voices offer plenty of clever suggestions, along with surprising case studies, techniques and strategies, the book is something much more than mere advice—it's a book of wisdom. The authors explain how the best leaders become talent magnets, the sort of people who attract the innovators and the high-achievers. And here's the cool part: you don't get there by just being a better boss; you get there by being a better person."

~ **Dale Dauten,** founder of The Innovator's Lab, syndicated columnist, and author of *Experiments Never Fail: A Guide for the Bored, Unappreciated and Underpaid* and *The Gifted Boss: How to Find, Create and Keep Great Employees*

"The opening chapter of *The Leader and The Coach*, entitled, 'What Just Happened?' is one of the most concise, pithy, and insightful assessments you'll ever read about remote work, our new life/work awareness, the Great Resignation—and the impact of what has emerged as a global paradigm shift. This alone is worth the price of the book... it is a must read for nascent and seasoned leaders, and for all who coach them."

~ **Alex Cyrell,** serial entrepreneur, co-founder and former CEO of Evercast, LLC

"Will Keiper and Steve Chandler break the mold in this timely, no-nonsense leadership book. Will provides great insights on how to be an effective leader in an environment requiring a commitment to greater empathy. Steve takes Will's practical and paradigm-shifting leadership strategies and offers real-world examples and common-sense coaching approaches to help every leader, and coach, raise their games."

~ **Mark Samuel,** CEO of IMPAQ and best-selling author of *Reimagine Teams: The Missing Piece in Team Building to Achieve Breakthrough Results*

"The blending of Will and Steve's perspectives and experiences and storied skill sets, brings to light the importance and necessity of 'leading with some feeling' in today's world. It isn't just 'nice,' but 'necessary' for keeping the best people and growing them. This book succinctly makes the case for why 'old school' managers must shift their approaches to create effective workplace relationships."

~ **Jeff Holtmeier,** Executive Chairman, Cinnova Technologies, Managing Partner of GENext, and founder of China-US Development Corporation

"Where's the opportunity? That's the question that renowned coach Steve Chandler asks readers of *The Leader and The Coach.* For anyone who coaches business leaders, as I do, this book contains wisdom to advance your coaching skills and, in turn, elevate your leader (and other) clients. This book is also an opportunity to learn from a seasoned CEO (co-author Will Keiper), who successfully evolved his coaching skills rather than succumb to a potentially career-ending event. The interplay between them ultimately reveals that neither role can fully succeed without the skills of the other."

~ **Lisa Conners Vogt,** MBA, ACC, CPC, Ever Better Coaching & Consulting

"A compelling and beneficial read and a great addition to both leaders' and coaches' playbooks. Steve and Will share compelling stories and personal experiences to illustrate the synergy between what might be seen as paradoxical: leadership and coaching. This timely book lights up new perspectives on leadership in the 21st century."

~ **Osama Al-Mosa,** MCC, ICTA, Senior Leadership Development Consultant, Amman, Jordan

The
LEADER
&
The
COACH

The Art of Humanity in Leadership

STEVE
CHANDLER

WILLIAM
KEIPER

FirstGlobal® Media LLC

The Leader and The Coach

Chris Nelson, Editor
Brannan Sirratt and Elisa Tidswell, Editorial Contributors
Carrie Brito, Cover Design

Imprint: FirstGlobal© Media LLC (contact publisher@firstglobalmedia.com)
Steve Chandler contact: www.stevechandler.com
Will Keiper contact: www.theleaderandthecoach.com

Library of Congress Control Number: 2022909684
ISBN-13: 978-0-9913835-4-2
First Edition

Table of Contents

Introduction

The Art of Humanity in Leadership

Leaders are human beings—always have been, always will be. Yet, despite this undeniable fact, accommodating holistic humanness as a principal factor in leadership has historically not been the top priority. Instead, the focus has been on market impact, financial results, and the continuity of the organization, which of course, are essential. But these are the outcomes of leadership, not the essence of it.

Followers have long accepted many stoic, top-down, directive, and depersonalized leadership styles—and still do in many places. This type of leadership often includes keeping work life a separate endeavor from the pursuit of greater well-being.

In *The Leader and The Coach,* we explain why the "old school" approaches have become outmoded in many parts of the world, and why some of the individuals most valued by organizations have concluded that working with approachable and enlightened leaders is no longer a mere hope.

A McKinsey study that included 18,000 people in fifteen countries addressed how workers might "future-proof" their skills and attitudes to be more valuable today and tomorrow.[1] The report stated that "... all citizens will benefit from having a set of foundational skills that ... add value beyond what can be done by automated systems and intelligent machines, operate in a digital environment, and continually adapt to new ways of working and new occupations." These are distinctly human capacities.

The study referenced several attributes that enable the presence of a higher degree of "humanness" in the workplace. Being empathetic, inspiring trust, showing humility, and offering more sociability in the "work" context, were among them. In addition, skills relating to inclusiveness, collaboration, empowerment, conflict resolution, and coaching were identified as of high value.

Leaders must embrace these more humanistic attitudes and skills and model them for their team members. It will likely feel uncomfortable and inconsistent with what may have worked in the past. But this reality cannot be ignored or left until there is "more time."

Simply put, the best leaders of today and tomorrow must infuse their leadership with some feeling. Unfortunately, seeing leaders offer this deeper dimension

---

[1] https://www.mckinsey.com/industries/public-and-social-sector/our-insights/defining-the-skills-citizens-will-need-in-the-future-world-of-work The research identified a set of 56 foundational skills that "will benefit all citizens and showed that higher proficiency in them is already associated with a higher likelihood of employment, higher incomes, and job satisfaction."

of their humanity has long been the exception—perhaps even considered a liability. Even enlightened leaders may still be uncomfortable using the words "feeling" and "our organization" in the same sentence.

The leaders who accept this shift in expectation and bring consciousness to the development of new attitudes and leadership skills will have a leg up in creating effective relationships beyond "leader" and "follower." These connections can promote individual growth and performance, the purpose and well-being of the organization, and the synergies between them.

Seeing and hearing team members as wholly human goes beyond talent attraction and retention. It is the type of openness that astute and courageous leaders can evoke to improve communication and collaboration, enhance creativity, and achieve greater prosperity.

Our experience has shown us that a leader with skill at coaching a whole person—acknowledging their body, mind, and spirit—will be able to attract, develop, retain, and optimize the talent of their people. We believe leaders with traditional skills who embrace the humanness that is the foundation of successful coaching can create powerful transformations for individuals, teams, and themselves.

We will explore these opportunities from the perspectives of a leader and a coach of leaders. Will Keiper, the Leader, offers his views from experience working as a CEO of NASDAQ, NYSE, and private organizations and as a professional business advisor. Steve Chandler, the Coach, is a renowned coach of leaders and leadership coaches. He gained his coaching expertise through working with executives and teams in over thirty Fortune 500 companies and with thousands of individuals and coaches.

Whether you are the CEO of a Fortune 500 company or a local hardware store, an executive director of a non-profit or the president of a school board, a Girl Scout volunteer leader or a high school sports coach, a pastor or parent—or the coach of one; the time has come for new approaches in developing the people and culture for which leaders are responsible. In *The Leader and The Coach* we will further explain why this is the case, why now, and introduce some pragmatic and readily actionable ways to create your own "humane" leader shift.

Steve Chandler, Birmingham, MI
William Keiper, Portland, OR

Summer 2022

The greatness of humanity is
not in being human, but in
being humane.

~ Mahatma Gandhi

One

"What Just Happened?"

Leader
[Will Keiper]

Early in my career as a leader, I repeated something I had heard other bosses proudly say: "The most important assets in our organization walk in and out of this building each day." Though feeling good about myself for saying those words, looking around the room at some of those "assets" I would see polite half-smiles, slowly nodding heads, and perhaps some sidelong glances. My words didn't ring true with them or me.

At the time, I viewed those human "resources" as somewhat fungible. Consistent with that view, I made it a practice to hide most forms of compassion from them. I knew that a day might come when it would be necessary to have a difficult conversation about performance improvement or even termination. I am ashamed to admit that I selfishly didn't want to feel badly because I knew too much about them personally. It was about protecting myself from having feelings that might be uncomfortable.

I also avoided lunches and dinners with the "troops" whenever possible. This was simply another way I isolated myself from "the most important assets in the organization." Although I lived this arm's-length approach longer than I care to admit, I finally recognized that it was not serving the organization, the people in it, or me. So, I started down the path of transformation, which I will describe in more detail ahead.

Today, these remnants of old-school leadership approaches stick out like sore thumbs. You can look around and see this for yourself. The constant, of course, is that humans remain fallible but capable of extraordinary transformation. Such shifts often come about when significant sea changes turn the comfort zone of the status quo into a danger zone. It is clear from today's more powerful and variable currents that staying the same is no longer optional. The time has come for expressing compassion as an essential element of effective and balanced leadership.

"Wait! I'm not ready yet."

The rise of the humanity factor in leadership has been underway for decades. But, as with most evolutions, the moves towards recognizing it as a leadership "must-have" were almost invisible for a long time. However, since the arrival of the new millennium, we have witnessed an explosion of change factors that turned this gradual shift into a rapid, large-scale phenomenon.

Imagine that you laid down for a nap on New Year's Day 2000, and Rip van Winkle-like, awakened today.

You would have slept through an unprecedented period of knowledge expansion and economic growth, the extraordinary rise of digital technology, major medical breakthroughs, the wake-up call of a viral pandemic, and striking shifts in wealth concentration.

Just since the first day of the 21st century, the top ten companies in the world (by market value) were displaced by the likes of Apple, Microsoft, Alphabet (which owns Google), Amazon, and Meta (formerly Facebook). As of this writing, only one non-technology company is in that group.: Berkshire-Hathaway—and it has significant investments in several of the companies just mentioned.

During this historically speaking quite short period of time, the brand names of breakthrough products and services became internationally renowned: the iPod, Skype, Facebook, YouTube, Twitter, Nintendo Wii, the iPhone, the iPad, Amazon Kindle, and Wikipedia, to name a few.

Google delivered an incredible organizational and search scheme for locating website locations and content. This tool made it possible for anyone to navigate the online universe. Since then, this technology platform has been chief among the enablers of global knowledge expansion and accessibility.

The rise of a parallel online world and social "community" changed our society across all generations. Changes in the world of work and organizational management were just as profound. Technologies made many once human-dependent tasks obsolete. Top talent became accessible across the globe. As a prime example, at the time of this writing, five of the top ten global technology companies are run by Indian-born CEOs, including Apple, Alphabet, and Microsoft.

Along came COVID-19

As if the digital technology tsunami wasn't a sufficient challenge over the past twenty-plus years, we also contended with the 9/11 terrorist attacks, the Great Recession, numerous wars, significant environmental degradation, climate disasters, and rising social and political polarization. These and other disruptive events and circumstances all across the globe became so frequent, that many of us became numb to them, no matter the human and financial tolls on those directly impacted.

Then came COVID-19, a pandemic affecting most parts of the world. Investors, business owners, and managers were quickly overwhelmed with significant, unexpected new challenges in traditional workplaces and markets served.

Many organizations had to urgently assess approaches that had long been in the "tried and true" category. Among them were the value of brick-and-mortar offices, maintaining company headquarters in densely populated, high-tax, high cost of living locations, face-to-face office time, commuting via public transit, business travel, and many other paradigms.

Organizations quickly integrated digital video and other technologies, creating new kinds of connections between individuals and teams. These tools rapidly enabled the emergence of a more autonomous, independent, and often more productive "work from home" worker.

In the aftermath of the arrival of COVID-19, global unemployment rose to an estimated 180 million-plus.[2] As part of this, workers in the retail, hospitality, and transportation sectors were sidelined globally, reaching scores of millions.

Virtually overnight, adults of all ages were confronted with income and affordability challenges. Smart, experienced, but now displaced former executives, managers, and other skilled workers, found themselves chasing fewer opportunities and less income—and experiencing greater anxiety about the future.

The impact of COVID-19 accelerated growth trendlines in many sectors and organizations virtually overnight. For example, McKinsey estimated that ten years of forecasted e-commerce adoption was compressed into just ninety days.[3]

---

[2] https://news.un.org/en/story/2021/06/1093182
[3] "This isn't just an e-commerce acceleration — it's a massive shift in consumer behavior, the type that traditionally takes decades to achieve." https://www.forbes.com/sites/forbesbusinesscouncil/2021/12/29/covid-

Few were exempt from having to see the world in a different way. But, as we will explore, seeing things differently enables doing things differently.

The rise of "whole persons"

As these realities sank in and the pandemic grew longer and longer, something extraordinary happened. Both the employed and unemployed began challenging the transactional relationship representative of many workplaces. There was a chorus of questions, such as, "A paycheck isn't enough," and "I'm not sure I can keep checking my uniqueness and humanness at the door of my workplace." These kinds of considerations became a wildfire-like phenomenon, with tens of millions of workers reassessing their needs and priorities.

Somehow the feelings of risk and fear that had for so long kept people's identities divided into the "work me" and the "real me," began melting away. It became easier to see the separation for what is was: artificial. This was partly because there was no longer such a marked distinction between work and home life, as so many people were working from home.

Also, during the rise of COVID-19 to pandemic status, many people, young and old, believed they were facing their mortality in a starker way than ever—and there is nothing like a very real sense of your potential death to

---

19-accelerated-e-commerce-adoption-what-does-it-mean-for-the-future/?sh=31032ec449df

get you to re-evaluate your life.

In late 2020, a Pew Research Center survey of working adults found that two-thirds of them reported feeling uncomfortable returning to the office and 57 percent reported choosing to work from home due to concern over exposure to COVID. As one consequence of this fear of contracting COVID-19 in face-to-face environments, some of those in the still-employed category decided to quit rather than return to an office.

This was the beginning of what became known as the "Great Resignation." Just in America, over 47 million citizens voluntarily quit their jobs in 2021, according to the U.S. Bureau of Labor Statistics. One of the reasons was the perceived inadequacy of compensation, of course. But a shift of a different sort was underway. More than 25 percent of the respondents of a large McKinsey & Company survey also cited "uncaring/uninspiring leaders," "ureliable/unsupportive colleagues,' "lack of workplace flexibility," and "lack of support for health and well-being," as reasons.[4]

As for what their new world might represent, many had a simple but powerful revelation: "I want to be treated with greater care and concern."

And in what some called the "Great Retirement," tens of millions of people closer to retirement age left the

---

[4] https://www.statista.com/chart/27830/reasons-for-quitting-previous-job/ Importantly, this survey encompassed 13,382 respondents from six countries.

workforce altogether. This was attributed to the fact that older individuals were more susceptible to the potentially fatal outcomes from contracting COVID, as well as a desire to focus on priorities other than work. So, they were also expressing, "I'm ready to treat *myself* with greater care and concern."

It is perhaps ironic that the rise of the online world that put screens between us—and a pandemic that created greater physical distance among us—opened our hearts and minds to the desire for a deeper human connection. The importance of being seen, cared about, and supported in one's "humanness," became a global phenomenon.

Silver lining

By failing to recognize and appreciate the distinctive human side of colleagues and team members, leaders, in some (perhaps many) cases, missed opportunities to leverage the powers latent in humanness: compassion, empathy, creativity, and service, to name a few. These factors, when cultivated and—more importantly— effectively modeled and communicated by the leader, give rise to teamwork and more efficient and creative problem-solving. It so happens that these skills also support organizational adaptability and resilience in times of rapid change and disruption—which today is the state of things almost all the time.

The rise of the priority for greater humanness in the context of leadership is here today, for the foreseeable future, and likely well beyond it. And that's a good thing, despite the liminal discomfort.

While the so-called "soft skills" have not been broadly developed in many organizations—they are and have been for decades the heart of the work between leadership coaches and their clients. The integration of coaching methodologies along with leadership best practices, is a readily accessible path to meeting the expectations for greater authenticity and empathy in leadership.

However, it is art more than science. It is a creative process, not a formulaic one. This is the stock-in-trade of objective, skilled leadership coaches accustomed to coaching their clients as "whole persons." That is, in terms of body, mind, and Spirit.

Steve Chandler's leadership coaching perspectives, anecdotes, and voice in this book provide an insider's view of one-on-one coaching fundamentals for leaders. Leaders of even the largest and most complex global organizations are reaching out for these resources, along with legions of owners and leaders of small and medium-sized organizations.

Based on our experience, we know that there is a silver lining amidst the accelerating rate of change in our world. Serving "whole person well-being" represents a significant opportunity for leaders and organizations.[5]

---

[5] https://thriveglobal.com/stories/3-ways-to-create-a-whole-person-employee-well-being-program/

Those leaders who recognize this moment as ripe for "rehumanizing" their leadership approach will have a competitive advantage and a team ready for flexibility, resilience, and rapid adaptation when required. They will also raise the probability of retaining their best performers.

Two

Learning to Dance with Impermanence

Coach
[Steve Chandler]

In my younger years, I placed a lot of value on *acceptance*. In my recovery program for alcoholism and addiction (gratefully initiated and embraced by me many decades ago) we would say the famous prayer, "God grant me the serenity to accept the things I cannot change, the courage to change the things I can, and the wisdom to know the difference."

The work I did with my own coach, Steve Hardison, took this worthy prayer a step further. Rather than merely *accepting* the things I can't change (and those things are coming fast and furiously these days), I learned to *welcome* them and help my clients do the same.

Mere "acceptance" can suggest (to the ego, trying to cling to permanence) that change is an unwelcome intrusion, something to be stoically endured until "normal" comes back around. But if we constantly keep these two creative inquiries alive—"What's good about this?" and "How can I use it?"—curiosity comes to life again, the way it was when we were little children and couldn't help approaching everything with genuine interest and fascination.

"Where's the gift in this so-called problem?"
should become a go-to inquiry for most
coaching sessions.

"Yes, we can *create* the context!"

The great leadership teacher Werner Erhard says, "Context is decisive." Because context, for every situation, is ours to create within. Most people don't see that—or even want to see it. They believe context arrives with every situation as a built-in limiter and there's nothing they can do about it. When someone mentions a recent change, they say, "Oh, wow, that sucks!" or "Hey, that's cool!" Built-in! We all agree! But do we have to? No, we can create it from the viewpoint of opportunity.

Here's an example of context creation I used for coaches in my coaching school who were panicking about their careers when COVID-19 swept through the world. "I'm afraid that my potential clients will be less likely to hire me because of the pandemic and its imposing restrictions."

No, quite the opposite! People locked down in their homes, not traveling and racing around in an array of personal and professional pursuits, had more time to be coached over Zoom or phone. Not only that, but they had more solitude available for introspection about what they might want their professional lives and relationships to be like.

Moreover, the lockdowns and restrictions diminished in-person contact. But it turned out that people were secretly longing to interact with others. They were open more than ever before to having a life coach or a business coach (who ought to be the same thing) to talk to regularly.

The coaches who were fearful and trying to merely "accept" what they perceived as a wholly negative situation became more tentative and apologetic about their work. They even devalued it by reducing their fees for people they imagined would not welcome coaching in that troubled time—especially if it wasn't in-person.

Whereas those coaches who *welcomed* this change in circumstance and put it into the context of potential clients wanting and needing their services more than ever—those coaches created an upswing in their businesses. Most of the coaches I was working with kept reporting, "I've just had my best month ever."

This is not to ignore or diminish the massive suffering that COVID-19 brought about. But when my commitment remains steady to serve people and the world—and to make a sustainable living doing so—it is always more creative and powerful to look for opportunities to do *that* instead of going into hiding and assuming the role of a victim.

Seeing things differently

One leader I was coaching was wringing his hands and feeling oppressed and defeated by the pandemic's constraints on his previous way of doing business. He wasn't a "big fan" of video conferences and much-preferred meeting his best customers and critical employees, shaking their hands, looking them in the eye, and giving them a bear hug. He even thought his tradition of taking those people out to bars and restaurants after their business meetings was a vital component of maintaining his good relationships.

Awareness of impermanence and appreciation of our human potential will give us a sense of urgency that we must use every precious moment.

~ The Dalai Lama

We worked on his willingness to see "What's good about this new reality?" in our coaching sessions. He realized that being travel-free gave him more time to have meaningful conversations and connect more often and deeply with the people who mattered most to his business. Over Zoom and Skype and phone (once he got comfortable with them), he found he could connect with many people he didn't have time for before the pandemic.

"What if I lose my job?"

A high-tech manager I coached lived with a pervasive fear of losing his job. There was a lot of downsizing going on in his industry and company. The thought that he might be a victim of it became a fear that contaminated his days and ruined his sleep.

"Tell me about your fear," I said. "What are you afraid of?"

"I might lose my job," he said.

"What would happen to you if you lost your job?" I asked.

"I'd be devastated," he said.

I turned to the whiteboard on the wall and wrote "DEVASTATED" in big letters.

I asked him to think about the word haunting his negative imaginary future, not to mention his present-day mood and mindset. I reminded him that the word "devastate" means to ruin or lay to waste entirely. Like a home devastated by an earthquake or hurricane, it would be flattened and no longer exist.

Would he be devastated if he lost his job? No, he realized. He'd find another job. What would he actually be if not devastated? "Uncomfortable," he conceded. "Is there a chance you could find an even better job if you were willing to live with being uncomfortable for a while?" "Yes," he said. "It's a good possibility."

By replacing fear of the unknown with curiosity we open ourselves up to an infinite stream of possibility. We can let fear rule our lives or we can become childlike with curiosity, pushing our boundaries, leaping out of our comfort zones, and accepting what life puts before us.

~ Alan Watts

So, his fear-producing thought—"I'll be devastated if I lose my job"—was, after being in a safe coaching zone where he could look inward for the truth, no longer producing fear in him. Instead, he discovered that his "knowing" what would happen wasn't even true.

This process of being curious and practicing self-inquiry is one way of separating leaders from their worrying egoic mind and helping them relax and expand into their innate wisdom. This approach was made famous and accessible by the spiritual teachings of Byron Katie and is used by many coaches today, including me. With practice, this work can alter who the leader is *being* in their unique circumstances: the owner of their life.

Instead of a fragile, vulnerable, little ego, a leader chooses to be seen as more fully human, experiencing their real being as a larger, wiser, and more creative energy field—a whole person, leaning into and even thriving on change.

Three

Successful Leadership Begins with Alignment

Will

My most successful and rewarding performances—as an individual and in my roles as a leader and professional advisor—have been when my beliefs, thoughts, words, and actions were in alignment. Establishing the foundation for this alignment required the thoughtful development of unique-to-me leadership principles. I view it as the core of an individualized leadership strategy that is aligned with the specific organization's purpose and resources.

A leadership strategy

Why is this important? First, it requires sorting the universe of possible choices. If you are a new leader or haven't yet articulated your fundamental values, this process will establish what you stand for. It is the equivalent of your Top Ten list of what's essential in pursuing the organization's strategy and purpose—specifically with you at the helm. Another leader's principles will be different (though there will likely be some in common as core to all successful leadership).

Second, a clear leadership charter enables you and your team members to be held accountable to the principles in a way that is blameless—not personal.

Third, these principles represent the framework for one-to-one and collective operating agreements within the organization. As your associates learn your principles and apply them in the organization's operation, a common vocabulary and approach to communication will develop.

Fourth, the presence and continuous affirmation of these principles are empowering for both the leader and the team.

Your principles will become the linchpins for everyone in the organization to rapidly and confidently adapt to situational disruptions and changes. As a result, the members of the team will have the equivalent of guidance "in advance" and can feel safer, more grounded, and more confident in taking autonomous action when possible. Enabling a greater degree of self-management is one measure of enlightened leadership.

No guessing required

Whenever I lead a company, coach organizations, or mentor individual leaders, I share my leadership principles with them. I use these to establish high-level performance guidelines (or to teach them how to do so in their specific leadership contexts). In simple terms, these "platform planks" represent what matters most to me and what is generally "okay" and "not okay" within my leadership scheme.

Here are my ten primary leadership principles:

Do what you say you will do.

This phrase simply means "honoring your word." It is the anchor agreement I give and expect. If each person consistently honors their word, integrity becomes part of the DNA of the team. And acting with integrity begets trust. It has the added value of clarity of measurement. What could be a better after-action review than this? "Yes, I did what I said I would do, and by the time I said I would do it." [6]

Prioritize cultivation of human capital.

We recognize and value each team member as a unique and precious asset. We agree that human-centered principles, such as trust, empathy, integrity, and authenticity, are core to our culture. Look for opportunities to practice these principles in your day-to-day performance. When you witness examples of these principles in action, take the time to notice and acknowledge the individuals for their contributions.

Be accountable for actions and outcomes.

Accountability for actions and outcomes is acting as

---

[6] For a complete explanation, see, Erhard, Werner and Jensen, Michael C., Creating Leaders: A New Model 11 Years On (May 8, 2014). Available at SSRN: https://ssrn.com/abstract=2434250

an "owner." Overt expression of ownership grounds performance agreements at the level of the individual. For example, "I understand that I am accountable for this work. I own these resources, challenges, and the outcomes. I will deliver."

Develop and deliver thoughtful and complete solutions.

For each instance where accountability is necessary, an agreement should be spelled out between the team members involved that results in: clearly describing the work/situation; directly or indirectly tying it to the purpose of the organization; establishing a time for completion; creating and evaluating potential actions and outcomes, and recommending a decision, with the rationale clearly explained.

Add value when and where possible.

Actively listen and weigh in when you have something of value to offer. Doing so is an indication of your commitment to organizational outcomes. It could be as simple as asking a timely question. We notice when team members make an effort to contribute outside their usual "lanes."

Take intelligent risks.

We expect and welcome thoughtful risk assessment and decision-making. Risk avoidance is impossible in an organization intent on building a core capability of rapid adaptation. This quote from Helen Keller explains why:

"Security is mostly a superstition… Avoiding danger is no safer in the long run than outright exposure."

Challenge the status quo.

We celebrate when people show the courage to challenge existing methods and assumptions. Through purposeful challenge and thoughtful reinvention of the status quo, we choose our future before it is forced on us by factors outside the organization.

No surprises.

Act on or surface potential issues or problems when you identify them. Typically, the earlier we notice smoke, the better we can prevent or manage a fire. Another way of avoiding surprises is this: when you find yourself unable to do what you've said you'll do within the agreed upon time, make this known the moment you realize it.

Turn mistakes into learning.

Making mistakes is unavoidable. Acting in integrity means acknowledging and owning them. It also means unpacking what happened so the team can learn from it and thereby build strength. Then, seek ways to improve the systems rather than placing blame or passing the buck.

Measure performance.

How are we doing? I like how Nike puts this, "We measure to get better, not just to keep score." We welcome opportunities to improve systems of measurement—key performance indicators for each area and individual, where possible. Shoot for objective, quantifiable measures.

These are the elements that are the context for *my* leadership. Yours will be a unique creation and should change over time to reflect your personal evolution and the new requirements you may confront. Always be asking, "What is my True North as a leader?" It is not okay to not know or be unable to continuously provide relatable examples. You may point out in a mentoring moment, "This is a great example of having the courage to take an intelligent risk." Recognizing people for doing things consistent with the leadership principles is the best way for the words to come to life.

Ad hoc situational responses are a poor substitute for clarifying how you expect the organization to reach agreements. A big part of your leadership persona could be left to chance if you cannot articulate your philosophy nor demonstrate a commitment to it.

The wisdom of a talent strategy

The Predictive Index surveyed 600 executives across twenty industries to understand their views of talent strategy—the relationship between talent optimization and organizational performance.[7] While most organizations reported that people are their highest expense and most valuable asset, only a very small percentage indicated that they had a talent strategy integrated with their business strategy.

Why is this, in my opinion, a mistake? Attracting high-performing people to any endeavor is challenging. Keeping them is even more difficult. The replacement of high performers is an enormous drain on time, energy, and money. And that is before considering the impact on the organization's functioning; it is nearly impossible to improve organizational performance with average performers.

A purposeful approach to talent development and management is as important as the strategy for achieving the mission and purposes of the organization, the leadership principles described earlier in this chapter, and the continuous measurement of the organization's performance and well-being. Leaders intent on leveraging competitive differentiators will exploit the synergies among these foundational elements of their leadership.

Although an organization's unique purpose will underpin its talent strategy, there will be some

---

[7] https://media.predictiveindex.com/legacy/wp-content/uploads/2020/01/TO_Benchmarking_Report.pdf Of the 600 senior leaders surveyed, 200 held the role of CEO or president. The remaining 400 were SVPs, VPs, or other members of the executive team.

commonalities. For example, a talent strategy should consider all these elements: sourcing and recruiting, selection, onboarding, training and development, engagement, career management, team development, performance management and measurement, rewards, and recognition.

A deep understanding of the basics of hiring and retaining key talent is not in every leader's wheelhouse. Therefore, leaving the specifics to the "experts" may be tempting. However, a committed leader cannot leave the management of this significant investment in people exclusively to others. And consider: if you can guide your organization to be among the few with business *and* talent objectives aligned, you could have a significant marketplace advantage.

As in many leadership situations, coaching can help remove a leader's blindfold of biases and limitations relating to talent. As a coach guides a leader in expanding their empathy in ways we discuss in this book, they will be able to assimilate those techniques into their approaches to all aspects of their leadership.

Greater engagement with and cultivation of talent serves productivity, teamwork, happiness, self-awareness, affiliation, recognition, attraction, and retention. For leaders committed to operational and financial success through expanding their humanness, this is an excellent reason to invest in self-development.

Four

Coaching "Who Am I Being?"

Steve

Whether or not their specialty is coaching leaders, every coach I know ends up coaching one sooner or later. But unfortunately, many are intimidated when that happens, believing that organizational leaders have rare and complex issues and knowledge beyond the scope of a coach not experienced in that specific world.

If you're in that situation, be reminded of the differences between coaching and consulting: Consulting is a process that often features specialized, expert advice, whereas coaching (at its best and highest level of functioning) opens the client up to personal insights and new possibilities.

Many coaches who are coaching leaders for the first time make the mistake of awkwardly trying to be a consultant. They want to help "fix" a specific problem instantly. Sometimes they want to appear knowledgeable beyond what they know, when "what they know" (how the mind works) is why the client is there. They don't realize that the client's insights and consequent transformation through personal coaching run deep and often last a lifetime.

Coaches make the most significant difference in a

leader's professional life when they focus on the player within the context of the game—not just the game.

When coaches bring attention and clarity to shifting a client's perceptions of failure, weakness, and "doing something wrong" into opportunities for increased curiosity and creativity, coaching value is highest.

Meditating upon the "shift" Will Keiper has insisted leaders can and should make to be both effective and personally fulfilled, I asked myself, "As a coach, how can I best guide a leader in making that shift?"

My answer was to take each of Will's ten leadership principles and offer some thoughts about how I would coach a leader to embrace them and put them into practice. These are my answers and some of the methods all coaches can consider employing:

Do what you say you will do.

Most leaders underestimate the power of their word. They are careless with their "promises" and unmindful of what happens when what they cannot be trusted to do what they say they will do. They have no idea what that behavior does to morale. It's hard to lead when people see the leader as out of integrity.

Coaching towards greater integrity works best when focused on its positive power. You want your leader-client to feel the added energy created when consciously honoring their word. You can help raise your client's awareness of when they are doing what they said they would do, being where they said they would be when they said they would be there, and when they are not.

It's enlightening and even thrilling when a leader (or any client) learns to "be their word." It has an almost intoxicating feeling of speaking one's world into existence.

Prioritize cultivation of human capital.

A coach can help leaders improve and increase their respect, care, and concern for the people who work with and for them.

Together we discover the power of recognition, encouragement, compassion, and respect for each "whole person" with whom the leader communicates. Can we elevate that respect to a deeply committed, consciously purposeful way of being? Assisting in converting my client's intentions (hoped-for behavior) into commitments (that can be trusted and counted on) is one of the great joys of coaching.

Be accountable for actions and outcomes.

When coaching a leader who habitually shifts blame and accountability when things don't go well, I will help them see that this behavior is toxic and unsustainable. It may be human and familiar, but it will undermine and subvert any desire they have to be an influential and respected leader.

When my client sees the positive benefits of learning to take responsibility for their actions and outcomes, it often leads to a course of exhilarating personal reinvention. As with almost all successful coaching experiences, the client will be encouraged to loosen their grip on their former fixed identity, accept and eventually welcome how changeable their habits can be. The leader's self-defensive ego loses its fear-based control over the leader's life and old way of being.

Deliver thoughtful and complete solutions.

Some of the leaders I coach communicate poorly. They deliver hasty, abrupt, and often unclear messages to their people. They do this almost without any forethought. When I point out that their words are often confusing or even offensive to the recipients of their communication, they become defensive and say, "I said what I meant. It's their problem if I didn't say it they way they wanted me to."

"No, it's your problem," I say, "but that's good news. You can improve it if you're open to an alternative approach."

Communication has two equally important aspects: First, how it gets said, and second, how it gets heard. Quite often those are two different things. If a leader is only concerned and responsible for how a message gets voiced, then there will always be communication issues. But once the leader also takes responsibility for how the communication lands, matters improve very quickly.

As a coach, I'll sometimes help a leader create the wording and tone of a communication. We'll evaluate how it could feel to receive it. And if it's appropriate, the leader might also check in with the recipients of the message: "How did this come across? Do you have questions or feedback?"

Add value when and where possible.

Some leaders I've coached have said, "It's not my way" to give praise and acknowledgment to other people. Wanting to be seen as tough old goats who are hard to impress is often the reason for this resistance.

And yet the value of positive reinforcement as a motivator has been proven. If the people you are leading feel seen, appreciated, and acknowledged, their morale and inclination to do better work increases.

So, do you want to get better as a leader, or is holding on to that old goat persona essential? When I'm coaching a leader like this, I want them to be open to the possibility that these practices would benefit their performance and level of influence. I don't want to make what they're doing "wrong," because it's not. It's just not as effective as another way of communicating would be. We can start the practice stage if I can help them see that the new habit aligns with their own goals.

Take intelligent risks.

Most people, leaders included, often associate uncertainty with fear and picture worst-case scenarios far more catastrophic than they would likely be if they ever came to pass. In coaching a leader who fears making an innovative and courageous decision, my role is to create a safe space to explore the potential pros and cons of the choices. In my role as the client's coach and thinking partner, no solution must be off the table.

The rapport and confidence created in the coaching relationship must convey to my client that my listening is non-judgmental and open to any feelings that come up, especially around fear and risk.

Sometimes brainstorming a workable Plan B if the risky choice fails to work can give the leader more confidence. Having a thinking partner helps in these cases. People have more courage than they realize, and I've often said that the simplest definition of what it means to coach is "to encourage." In a coaching context, the word encourage means to help someone find the courage that's already there but hidden.

Challenge the status quo.

My coach taught me to challenge my life's status quo, especially my career. He taught me to always be tapping into the divine and limitless nature of human creativity. He did this by asking—no matter what situation I presented him with, how scary the opportunity or how bad the problem was—"What would you like to create?"

That ongoing line of inquiry changed my life and career in remarkable, unforgettable ways. And I've adapted my version of his process to apply to leaders (and anyone else) I coach.

Tell me your status quo, and I'll ask you if it is working for you. Even if you say yes, I'll ask how you might improve it. How could you make it radically different and better? What would you like to create? Why is "good enough" good enough for you? What's possible? You're telling me what this business is like now, but I want to know what you want it to *become*.

No surprises.

I once heard a successful leader tell me, "What separates a great leader from a good leader is that great leaders tell the truth sooner."

Some leaders I have worked with seemed to get a sense of power and privilege by hoarding information and keeping secrets that would have been helpful for everyone to know. They might say, "I'll tell them when I'm ready. They can't handle the truth right now."

Coaching a leader away from passive-aggressive, punitive, and judgmental thinking can create more trust and respect. The same for creating a policy of open communication and immediate information sharing. One of my clients was so happy with the results of developing that habit that he had a sign on his office whiteboard that said, "Communication solves all problems." That might not be literally true in all cases, but it was true enough to keep him on the path of no surprises.

Turn mistakes into learning.

One of my public relations clients from long ago was Dick Tomey, then-head football coach for the University of Arizona. After a game in which his team won, I noticed that he never looked pleased. I asked him why that was, and he said, "We never learn anything when we win. We get cocky. When we lose, we learn and grow better."

When clients are upset about mistakes made, my role as a coach is to invite them to run what I call "game film." on the error. Just as professional sports teams watch the film of their previous game to see where they can improve in the games ahead, a coaching game film review is designed to take the negative emotion out of the "mistake" and transform it into a learning opportunity.

It's vital for the coach to help the client see that this isn't just some kind of positive thinking spin or "reframing" to paper over a bad situation—rather it's an inquiry that can transform the "mistake" into an actual learning experience.

Measure performance.

Early in my career as a seminar leader working with leadership and sales teams, I feasted on the wisdom of two impactful books, The Great Game of Business by Jack Stack and The Game of Work by Charles Coonradt. The message that came through them is that performance rises whenever you introduce and then increase the game element. People play games with more enthusiasm and innovation than they do the dull grind of "work."

And, counter-intuitively to me at the time, one powerful way to do that is by sharing and highlighting the numbers—keeping score, measuring, and celebrating performance so that the whole team knows where they stand on any given day.

When coaching leaders, I like to explore how the numbers are shared and how team members are playing full-out to improve the score. With coaching, the point is not to make hidden numbers and unmeasured performance wrong. Instead, coaching needs to encompass exploration, discovery, and possibility.

Clients are sometimes resistant to giving up their long-held beliefs about how leadership should work. But good coaching will not seek to persuade a client to replace one view with another. Instead, when the conversation is one of, "Could you be open to the possibility...?" progress can happen faster and more effectively. "Could you be open to the possibility that more and better performance measures could lead to even better results?"

Five

Leader Shift

Will

Some of the leadership factors we offer for your consideration are different than they once were. But the principal challenge for a leader hasn't changed. "Given today's context, how do I best guide and motivate my team from where we are to where we need to be?"

This crossing could be a once-in-a-lifetime opportunity to bring more of your humanity to various life roles, including leadership. The irrefutable logic behind the rise of "whole personhood" is that we are shortchanging ourselves by numbly checking our humanity at the doors of our "work lives." As with most significant organizational shifts, the leader should be showing the way toward this freedom.

You first

The changes ultimately seen by others begin with the internal transformation desired, sought, and achieved individually. The transformation of any person and any leader is an effort in "becoming."

The leader's role should be to explain and model the humanity and mindfulness that can raise the level of the culture. Unfortunately, or perhaps more aptly, fortunately, this will require a move into the discomfort zone, where most growth and change occur.

Is leadership more effective with much of our individuality hidden behind remoteness? Ask yourself, "Would I be more effective as a leader by revealing more of my humanity? My authenticity, self-awareness, creativity, compassion, hopes, and fears, who and what I love, and my desire for connection?" If you could be more effective (let alone happier), isn't it time to challenge the old beliefs about what a leader is and how they should show up to the best effect?

This is not to say that "command and control" wasn't, isn't, and can't be, a viable and successful leadership approach. Also, in parts of the world with cultures that reinforce the "I'm the leader and you're a follower..." approach, it currently may be impossible to break out of that established and still-accepted formula. In authoritarian and male-dominant societies (and in most military organizations), greater expression of individual uniqueness can be anathema to the desired culture.

But social media and the shrinking of the globe are two elements that suggest it may not be too early to learn something about what the workers and team members may be thinking and feeling in those cultures. Remember the developments and outcomes of the Arab Spring, for example?[8]

---

[8] https://en.wikipedia.org/wiki/Arab_Spring#

Who knows what might develop in the rest of this century, and where? As a first step, perhaps there could be some hybridized forms of the traditional command and control leadership style with the intention of more significant human connection between leadership and team members.

Overdue questions

Isn't it the best use of our lives to grow into our full potential as humans by breaking out of limiting beliefs? In all our roles?

In many parts of the world, showing greater humanity in leadership and achieving agreed-upon results have become inextricably intertwined. So how did we come to this moment, beyond the external drivers reviewed earlier?

Remote work eliminated the separation of the workplace from the rest of life in physical and psychological terms. Workers had to process this new way of operating, for the most part, independently (or in consultation with co-workers) rather than with the boss. As a result, they learned to work with greater autonomy and personal accountability, and for many, confidence grew.

Today, you might hear from an associate, "How can I have greater flexibility in my workstyle?" As the leader, you might need to consider, "How should we be organized now? How can I create a roadmap back," or,

"Should I shift in the direction of potential hybrid workstyles that might better suit our needs today?"

The independence associated with being remote from the office was empowering. Associates might now ask themselves, "Maybe I could do more at work or learn something new." "How will my work life be enriched if I am willing to increase my contributions?"

In turn, you as a leader might need to consider: "How can I accommodate and encourage this greater engagement and willingness to contribute?" "How might I refocus these revelations into new opportunities for expanding job roles, accountability, and incentives?"

For some team members, thoughts turned to joining the "independent creator" economy and envisioning realistic, even attractive, options. As the leader, you might contemplate, "How could our current business model integrate these kinds of options for those interested? What alternatives might be mutually beneficial for retaining this energy and creativity in our organization?"

On the other hand, the isolation of remote work made clear the loss of workplace connections and community. As a result, there was a rise in "burnout" and a more significant strain on emotional and mental health. Team members might now be asking, "What about opportunities to improve my physical health (nutrition, fitness, smoking cessation, weight loss) and mental health (depression, anxiety, burnout, and the 'diseases of despair')? I need some support."

As the leader, you might ask, "What can I do to address actionable well-being options now? Should I consider the team's input about priorities and what they are willing to contribute to these efforts?"

For some anticipating a return to an office, expectations rose along with a willingness to ask questions. "Will things be different now? What if they are or they're not? I want to understand why we do what we do and my specific role. I would like more input into the things that affect me."

There was time for considering what might be missing from the workplace that is a central part of life. For example, assume that some of your colleagues will ask, "Do I still feel good about the bargain here?" "I think my contributions are more valuable than I thought." And even, "This doesn't feel right."

The elements described all relate to the requirements and needs of the human resources, which in most organizations are the *essential* resources. Responding to them deserves the best thinking you have. It isn't about appearing "approachable" or "nice," although this is certainly desirable. It is about fighting for the continuity of the organization.

The best talent knows there are many places to spend their energy and creative abilities and feel valued and appreciated. They will be aware that there are leaders who embrace empathy as an advantage, not a burden, and are creating cultures that make this a reality for all concerned.

Answering the questions just suggested, and many more focused on the human elements in an organization, means that their leader cares about them beyond their functional value. It's a business and organizational competitive requirement today, not a nice-to-have. If this wave hasn't yet reached your place in the ecosystem of organizations—sooner or later, it will.

A leadership foundation for the times

Your team will need consistent, affirming messages that will anchor the purpose of the organization and their roles in it. Please consider creating communications that establish your "baseline narrative" for the organization's transformation into a more humane, adaptable, and resilient one. In your unique voice, this narrative should reflect current reality and aspirations. It should be frequently repeated and reinforced. Think of it as the backbeat of practical, consistent, transparent leadership.

The narrative can serve as the touchstone for leaders moving from a slow rate of change to a faster one. The leader should reinforce the narrative in affirming and reassuring ways so team members can see that "My leader is leading… and it's not off a cliff." Own it and make it a "living document," and make adjustments based upon what you learn along the way.

Here are a few specific concepts to consider:

Recognizing the "bigger picture" (another term for context) is essential.

The leader describes their awareness of events beyond the organization that may require changes. For example, "I am aware that disruptions in the external environment have and will continue to occur. Some of these will have implications for our organization and people, and we will prepare to address them."

Clarify and affirm the purpose of the organization.

"This is where we are going and why are we bound together." One survey found that employees are five times more likely to be excited to work at a company that knows why and how they impact the world. If the purpose is fuzzy, the leader must bring it into focus.

Commit to involving team members in the creation of this transforming organization.

Show the team members that your leadership is a "we" process, not an "I" process. This could start by simply using the collective terms "we," "us," and "our" whenever referring to the organization.

Describe how you view your current responsibilities and what the team can expect from you.

For example, "I am committed to..." and, "You can count on me for..."

Confirm that these adjustments are part of a process that won't end.

"We don't know what we don't know, and we will make adjustments based upon new knowledge and facts."

Describe the objective of raising the individual and overall sense of well-being.

Again, describe this as an ongoing process, not an event.

Ask for feedback on what you've said.

Take the time to listen. Take some notes. Tell your team you'll process what you've heard and suggest some first steps. You don't have to have answers for everything in the moment.

Six

Moving Toward Creation

Steve

The practices Will Keiper has just advocated for leaders moving away from authoritarian control to a more humane and mindful collaboration with all team members can potentially change cultures and productivity itself.

The contemporary Buddhist meditation teacher and author Shinzen Young often speaks of the ancient Indian sages who observed that the world has two kinds of people. By far the most common, the first kind of person sees every development as either good fortune or bad fortune. On the other hand, the rarer person is willing to see everything as an opportunity.

The good news here is that this opportunity-based viewpoint can be learned. It's not a fixed personality trait. It's a skill developed through commitment and practice. The changeability of personality traits and even the brain itself has been one of the most exciting breakthroughs in neuroscience and positive psychology. These breakthroughs are vital to leadership and coaching alike. And they were crucial for me.

One of the many benefits I have personally experienced from being coached is that my old habit of seeing every new circumstance as either bad fortune or good (mainly bad) was challenged by my coach. He would listen patiently and compassionately to my latest problem and hear the victimized context I was putting it in until I finally got it off my chest. At that point, he would invite me into the world of possibility, where he always seemed to come from.

"Are you willing to open up a bit and play with this?" he would ask.

Of course, I was. I was paying a lot for the coaching and wasn't about to hide out in denial during the sessions, no matter how uncomfortable these challenges felt at first.

He asked me if I was willing to see the gift inside the problem. He'd say things like, "What's good about this? Where's the opportunity?" And after a lengthy and creative brainstorm together, I would begin to see things that I couldn't see when I was locked in my small self, my victim self, and holding tightly to my self-created story of misfortune.

"What's good, here and now?"

The ancient Buddhist sages' path for moving away from the perceptions of the first kind of person (everything processed as good fortune or misfortune) was once thought to be discovered through years, even decades, of meditation. This process would (hopefully) culminate in "enlightenment" about accepting and enjoying the impermanence that is the nature of life.

I was not a meditator or a student of positive psychology in my early years as a coach. Still, I was fortunate to have a coach who was, so my version of "enlightenment" began to occur after a comparatively few coaching sessions with him. Of course, my new opportunity lens was temporary (on loan from my coach) and only directed at each particular "problem" as it appeared.

However, over time, when it kept happening again and again in sessions, it became a habit for me. When something troubling occurred, and before my coach asked me, I would ask myself, "What might be good about this?" and "How can I use this?" and then do a no-pressure creative brainstorm about how I could choose to respond to the new situation.

Over the years, my experience has verified that coaches and especially leaders can benefit from practicing a "What's good about this?" inquiry in each situation that arises.

When I do seminars with leaders and managers who sometimes question this practice as being an unrealistic sugar-coating of real problems, I remind them of the words of British Field Marshall Bernard Montgomery, He was one of the toughest and most effective military leaders in World War II. He said, "A leader must have infectious optimism. The final test of a leader is the feeling you have when you leave their presence after a conversation. Do you have a feeling of uplift and confidence?"

Too many leaders I've worked with seem unconcerned with whether their people leave a meeting uplifted or depressed and discouraged. What they are ignoring is the human factor. They are unconsciously downgrading the creative energy, morale, and potential of the very people they are counting on to deliver the goods.

Turn it around

I once went to my coach with a long-winded complaint about the leader of a high-tech company I was working for as an internal sales trainer. I told him that I viewed this guy as totally ineffective and dysfunctional as a leader. I said it was oppressive and suffocating to work under such a person. He listened sympathetically, but I thought it a bit strange that his eyes seemed to be lighting up at the same time.

"This is gold," he said.

By then, we'd done enough of these sessions for him to skip the "Are you open to a different possibility...?" part.

"Gold?" I asked. "What do you see in this that looks like gold?"

"Opportunity," he said. "I see an answer to the question, 'How can I use this?'"

My coach knew I had been creating and delivering seminars both inside and outside the company I was working for and was always looking for new material. He said, "This is what you were looking for. This is your leadership seminar."

"What . . . a seminar about how *not* to be a leader?"

"Yes," he said. "Wouldn't it be valuable for leaders and managers to know that?"

I suddenly saw what he meant. So I went home and wrote out the mistakes I thought my boss was making. Then I wrote out the different ways of being (showing up) that I thought would resolve those mistakes.

The seminar became a huge hit for leadership and management teams and was the foundation for my book *100 Ways to Motivate Others* which continues to sell quite well today, although it was written years ago.[9]

Opportunity and possibility

Having read Will's facts about the accelerating rate of change occurring in our world, you might be feeling it as a gut punch. It's tempting to process these significant changes and disruptions as misfortune landing on your head. But, of course, it's not just you who might feel daunted. The people who follow your lead (whether

---

[9] https://www.amazon.com/100-Ways-Motivate-Others-Third-ebook/dp/B07J1R8BW5/ref=sr_1_1?crid=27E5GFUETX267&keywords=100+ways+to+motivate+others&qid=1646946848&sprefix=%2Caps%2C217&sr=8-1

leader or coach) will likely have a very human adverse reaction to the changes occurring in our world today.

When I coach people who feel victimized by the "misfortune" of dealing with something new (such as having to conduct meetings by videoconference instead of in-person), I use the same lines of inquiry that my coach used with me. After fully acknowledging the discomfort, I elevate the conversation into the realm of opportunity and possibility, and right away the problem can be rechanneled into a creative project. This perceived misfortune is rapidly morphed into a seed of opportunity. This is the very shift that lives at the source of effective leadership today.

The only way to make sense out of change is to plunge into it, move with it, and join the dance.

~ Alan Watts

Coaches must shift too!

If you listened in on a coaching session I had with a leader today, you wouldn't recognize the work known as "coaching" compared to how I (and most other coaches) worked in the "old" days.

To illustrate the difference, where I used to coach "what to do and say" (the moves on the chessboard), today I focus more on what we have described as the well-being of the "whole person" (the chess player). As a result, my leader-clients can elevate their management skills in the same way. They're not just leading performance improvements (the moves). They are also focused on the well-being and personal growth of those directly responsible for the moves (the players, including themselves).

If this doesn't sound like rocket science, that's good—because it's not. But it requires a commitment that must be kept alive through conscious and purposeful renewal.

Seven

A Two-Way Street

Will

Creating a more evolved workplace is not a one-way street—not by a long shot. A leader is entitled to (and should) say, "To create a community of value, we must work together to build our individual and collective well-being in the context of our organization and its purpose. It must be a sustained, collaborative effort based upon agreements that go beyond job descriptions and operational requirements."

"We agree...."

Each team member must commit and engage more fully. Setting the course for this "community building" starts with the leader articulating some foundational agreements. Here are some suggestions for where to start:

Committing to the vision and purpose of the organization.

Each team member must understand the vision and purpose of the organization and how what they do ties into it. Team members must act and be "in"—not watching from the margins, or "out."

Adopting an owner's mentality.

Team members must treat their roles and responsibilities as though they are "owners," and as if their livelihood depends upon their commitment. (Doesn't it?)

Serving with integrity and transparency.

Each team member commits to consistently acting with integrity and transparency in their service to the leader, fellow team members, customers, and other constituents.

Being an active problem solver.

Each team member asks, "What can I do to better serve those around me?" as often as possible, and shows a bias for action.

Seeing others in the organization as "whole persons."

Team members must invest in personal outreach, greater openness, and understanding.

Seeking opportunities for growth and improvement.

Team members and the organization win when they enhance their expertise, skills, education, and ability to contribute. Committed team members will actively desire and act on this kind of ongoing self-development.

Making the call

A move toward greater collaborative and human-centric leadership is inevitable for organizations wanting to attract and keep the best talent. The aim of these firms is to become more resilient and adaptive "sur-thrivers" no matter the disruptions that arise.

But leadership at every level requires the making of many solo decisions and accepting full responsibility for the outcomes. As we have established, effective and responsible leadership calls for greater balance between performance and compassion. However, longer-term considerations for showing the way to greater well-being can be swamped by the urgent needs for survival in the short-term. There are times when this is unavoidable.

Making this clear to the team is another indication of the "leader as pragmatist." This might be expressed as, "From time-to-time it is part of my job to make timely decisions for which I alone must be responsible. There will be times I will need to make decisions with less than complete information, and even times when I cannot get the team's input. When these circumstances arise, I commit to making decisions in the organization's best interest."

Enlightened leadership includes knowing when responsibility cannot be delegated or put up for a vote.

Greater empathy and compassion as a part of a leader's persona and actions isn't reached through a single proclamation. It must be manifested through balancing outcomes and well-being day in and day out. It is "banked" over time through one-on-one conversations—both talking and listening with greater intention—so that when moments requiring decisive action arise, team members can understand them in context and trust the leader's judgment.

"Getting to fair"

I once served as the president of a franchise organization. When it was founded, the organization had a reasonable system of support for the franchise owners, and collected a royalty on their sales.

However, the business sector we were in very rapidly evolved. It became clear that the franchisees would have to develop their own unique "store systems" to serve their customers. The products and solutions they could offer were often determined by the accessibility of locally-available technical talent that could implement them for customers. We could not provide this service for them on a market-by-market basis, and national advertising as a value-added element was untenable. It became apparent to all (especially the increasingly frustrated franchise owners) that the relationship with us had to change or end.

We initially resisted giving up the royalty revenue that sustained the headquarters' organization and saw sales grow to more than $400 million per year. But most of the franchisees were active owner-operators who, in many cases, had their livelihood, life-savings, and family futures at stake. The value proposition on offer from us was no longer fair. Serving their interests was not only the humane thing to do but was our reason for being as an organization.

A crucial factor was that the accelerating technological changes and product advancements in our field made the assortment, availability, pricing, and timely delivery of the products an absolute requirement for franchisees to stay in business. They could acquire the products from many other suppliers.

The "human factor" tipped the balance in our favor, though I didn't recognize it at the time. We had created a community of hundreds of franchise owners. They attended numerous regional and national events during the year. They got to know each other and the support team at headquarters on a one-to-one basis. There were common challenges and solutions—business and personal. We saw one another as "whole persons" with a common purpose of creating a symbiotic organization for individual and collective success. It was business, *and* it was personal.

There were conversations with and among all constituents about the "how-to," but the headquarters' leadership had to make the ultimate "what" decision. We called upon our team to create a financial model that would replace our gross margins and profits from royalties with a "cost-plus" uplift on the products. We also asked the franchisees to consolidate more of their product purchases through us—requesting that they prefer us over alternative suppliers. Due to the personal relationships, along with a fair pricing model and service level, almost all of them stuck with us.

Ultimately it was a "blind corner" decision, the outcome of which could only be viewed after the turn was made. But with the support of franchise owners and the efforts of the HQ team, we made the revenue transition from royalties to cost-plus product sales in a single year. Royalties came down step by step while the "plus" part of the cost-plus product model was implemented and adjusted.

Over the succeeding four years, we grew our affiliated locations from fewer than 400 to over 1,400. During that period, our revenue tripled to over $1.5 billion, and we remained profitable throughout. Our franchisee colleagues were able to compete in their markets more effectively and grow.

It was a successful bargain, with all the parties doing what was required. In today's terms, it was a business solution intertwined with seeing each other as human and humane, and "getting to fair."

Eight

The Creative Power of Agreements

Steve

The most successful system I've found for helping leaders create and execute a process that keeps a team aligned and motivated is what I call "leading by agreement."

Without this system, leaders seem to default to leading by expectation. "Here's what I need and expect you to do."

Leading by expectation runs counter to the aversion most of us have to trying to live up to other people's standards. And that's assuming we even understand what the expectations are! Many leaders who are stingy with their communication leave their direct reports guessing what's expected of them.

But even when we know what the expectations are, it can still be uncomfortable and demotivating when we don't have a clue as to the "why" behind them. In many cases, an employee or team partner will be called onto the carpet for failing to live up to a leader's expectation, even if that expectation wasn't clear in the first place.

To illustrate this conundrum, I would often begin leadership and management seminars by helping attendees feel their own visceral rebellion against another person's "expectations." I would begin by saying, "I expect your full attention—no side conversations. I expect you to fill in your guidebooks as we go. I expect you to be back on time from the breaks we take." Although they accepted the expectations, no one looked very happy about how I was communicating with them.

When they were finished shifting around in discomfort, glancing at each other with a "Who does he think he is?" look on their faces, I took a long pause and shifted gears to agreements. "Do you all have your guidebooks in front of you?" Yes. "By a show of hands, will you agree to fill them out as we go?" All hands up. "Our next break will be in an hour, and it's for fifteen minutes. Can I get your agreement to be back in your place on time?" Yes. "Is there anyone here unable to agree to that?" No.

Then I invited them to give me feedback on how they felt when hearing me deliver my expectations of them versus how it felt when I asked for agreement. They said it was like night and day. And that's because it is.

Do you want to confront or create?

I once coached a leader who had a young employee (we'll call him Justin) who drove him crazy by turning work in late. There were reports due Friday that weren't getting in until Monday or Tuesday of the following week.

The leader "hated confrontation" but knew he needed to have a difficult talk to tell Justin how disappointed he was. He was thinking of putting him "on report" and letting him know his future in the organization would be short if he didn't become more reliable.

My client finally said he had procrastinated long enough on having that confrontation with Justin. I reassured him that procrastination is very common when the task ahead feels so unpleasant. I've met leaders who have procrastinated for months and years on necessary but "difficult" conversations with people who work for them, even though putting them off has led to a damaging loss of effectiveness, morale, and productivity, for them and the organization.

Fortunately, this leader had been in my workshop on leading by agreement. So, when I asked him about his problem with Justin and the tardy reports, he knew where I was going when I said, "What agreement is being broken?"

At first, he was silent and looked embarrassed. Finally, he said, "He knows that report should be in by Friday."

"Does he?" I asked.

"Well, he *should* know. He's supposed to be a professional. I can't babysit everybody or coddle people who are not doing their jobs."

"Do you and he have an agreement that is not being

kept?" I asked.

"He knows what I expect of him," he said.

My leader-client realized that he had defaulted back to the old mindset of leading by expectation. "That's not wrong," I reminded him. "It's just not very functional."

So, we worked out how his upcoming conversation with Justin could potentially have a positive outcome. It could be about creating a new, fully committed agreement. My client was now able to see this as a better alternative to calling Justin out for bad behavior and warning him that his job was not secure anymore.

A few days after our coaching session, he called me to say that the meeting went exceptionally well—and that when he worked with Justin to create a committed agreement, he found out that another department was often late in getting data to Justin that he needed to finish the report. My client told Justin he'd handle that, and Justin said he could promise and deliver on Friday under their new agreement.

Solving problems before they occur

When I'm coaching a leader who wants and *expects* buy-in from their people on the process they have put in place for hitting the team's goals, I ask how the buy-in will happen. They often tell me they plan to get the buy-in by giving a forceful talk about the process at a retreat or team meeting. Some others say they will deliver a strongly-worded memo outlining what's expected.

My next question is often, "And how is that working out for you so far?"

And their answer is, "It's, okay, it's so-so," or, "It's not that great."

In most cases, an essential consideration has been left out of the communication: the effect on the person hearing it! It requires genuine clarity for people to trust the process and execute their activities to support it. It's essential to get clear agreements on what those activities will be, how those agreements benefit the mission, and precisely which parties are involved in the agreement.

Agreements are creative by nature. It's two or more people designing a work of art together as a collaborative creation. Because it is a collaborative and creative process for both parties, the approach can be more relaxed, and even inspired. No more procrastination on getting systems started or corrected.

When leading by agreement, problems can be discussed and even eliminated before they happen. For example, if the leader I was coaching in the anecdote above had created his agreement with Justin the moment he gave the assignment, it would have saved a lot of unnecessary trouble and confusion for all concerned.

The default system of groups of all kinds, including marriages and families, is to live in the minefield of expectation. But clarity, performance, and productivity will rise through agreements rather than one-sided statements of expectation.

Nine

From Resistance to Awakening

Will

I once led a mid-sized software company that had developed a simple way for smaller businesses to network their computers. The solution, "peer-to-peer" networking, was reliable, affordable, and, as technology goes, friendly. Our market success was such that we were able to go public as a NASDAQ-listed company.

I awakened one morning to learn that our top two developers had decided to move to Microsoft. The good news was that their recruitment validated our solution and suggested that our "niche" market (from which we were then garnering annual sales of over $100 million) had more significant potential than we could have imagined. The bad news was that our survival was seriously in doubt.

Adapt or die

Unsurprisingly, Microsoft released a small office and home version of a peer-to-peer networking solution as a feature in the next release of the Windows operating system. This meant that software equivalent in large part to ours was included free in every PC shipped with Windows. Millions of them each year.

From the moment we lost our two key engineers, we knew that diversifying our product offerings would better serve our cause than attempting to fight Microsoft. Therefore, the fastest route to being more than a "one-trick pony" as a product company was to diversify our software solutions through acquisition.

We immediately got busy. We spoke with more than sixty small software companies whose offerings we thought could help extend our product line. We ended up acquiring two such companies.

During the same period, our sales declined (in anticipation of the release of the next version of Windows) to 50 percent of their prior level. All along the way, we were step-wise reducing costs, the largest of which were employee-related. As a result, we had no choice but to terminate more employees each quarter to keep our losses to a minimum.

Catching a falling knife

Employees continued to ask questions about whether there would be more terminations. I was afraid to say, "Yes, but I don't know how many and whether you might be among them," so I danced around the issues as best I could.

But I chose not to talk with team members individually about their concerns and didn't offer any reasons for not giving more insight. My justification (to myself) was that I didn't want to get too close to anyone, so there wouldn't be a human connection to color what I viewed as black-and-white financial judgments.

One day, my mentor and board member, Gary E. Liebl, suggested, "Why not explain why you are making gradual cuts rather than doing it all at once? Our objective has been and is to keep as many people employed as possible, for as long as possible." he said. "Let them in on it. It may not make it easier to accept the uncertainty, but they will know that their interests are first rather than not being thought about at all."

My fear had clouded my judgment of the right thing to do. In the next company meeting, I said, "The goal is to keep as many jobs as possible while staying as close to breakeven as we can during this uncertain period. If we don't do this, there may not be jobs for anyone." It was the unadulterated truth. I delivered the message with empathy, acknowledging the uncertainty this created for them and their families. I didn't detect a sigh of relief in the room, but there was an easing of tensions by knowing the truth.[10]

My awakening

The "opportunity" in this leadership experience was to wake-up to the necessity and value of empathy in

---

[10] The rest of the story is that we were able to rather quickly complete the acquisition of two software companies that successfully diversified the business. The organization still lives today, operating under another name, under solid leadership, and continues to employ skilled and dedicated people.

leadership, specifically mine. It opened my eyes to the power—and necessity—of an organizational community and team, not a boss and the troops.

I began looking deeply at my leadership foundation and found some essential aspects were underdeveloped: humanity, mindfulness, and authenticity, among others. My heart had to open, even though I was afraid. I had to learn to ask the people around me what they thought and then listen to, and truly hear, their inputs.

My reformation was a slow and sometimes uncomfortable process. But over time I began feeling greater freedom and a loosening of the armor I had worn for so long.

My study and learning about well-being, consciousness, and seeing others as "whole persons" deepened. I eventually opened to the value (and actions) embodied in concepts like "opening up," "psychological safety," "humanity," "empathy," "collaboration," and "enlightenment." I learned to share these with team members and other leaders. Something amazing happened.

My work became even more stimulating, and my connections with people were more energized. They welcomed my views on why and how they could integrate greater humanity into their work and leadership. I felt my sense of value soar by showing up more authentically.

This embracing of humanness has become an integral

part of my living, business consulting, and leadership coaching.

Ready or not

It would be difficult to find a person nowadays unaware of the power shift in the direction of the employee, worker, or team member. Or the increased value placed upon "workstyle" as a big part of an individual's overall lifestyle. Or the link between the workplace and the psychological needs for belonging, collaboration, recognition, and perhaps, in context, feeling loved. The top talent you need to attract and retain understands that greater humanity and well-being in the workplace are today's table stakes.

And the day came when the risk to remain tight in a bud was more painful than the risk it took to blossom.

~Anaïs Nin

Every leader has had to deal with change management in some form, and most have learned that it is a process, not an event. Rather than objecting to a "loss of power" or the "misfortune" that Steve has discussed, this could be a moment to be a creator. To ask instead, "What's the opportunity here? Where's the gold? What if I seized the moment to openly acknowledge both the challenges and the opportunities for greater connection, collaboration, and deliberate mindfulness as a part of my leadership?"

Ten

Rising Above the Blame Game

Steve

I learn a lot from the people I coach, especially the leaders.

However, that wasn't always the case because I didn't listen all that well in the early stages of my coaching career. I was so insecure about my credibility and worthiness as a coach that I did far too much teaching, advising, and judging. As a result, I did too much telling.

I have since learned that people like me do that from an insecurity. We try to "fix" other people we see as doing things wrong.

I lost at least half of my impact as a coach by not listening. I spoke advice and communication techniques to ears that could not hear what I was saying. I hadn't taken the time to understand what was really going on with them. I couldn't see or hear the fears and beliefs blocking them from being who they wanted and needed to be.

I was often prescribing things to do that were premature for them or downright inappropriate. I was like a doctor prescribing amphetamines for insomnia.

But once I started listening, I started learning.

Every system is a perfect system

One of the most life-changing learning experiences I ever had was during the years I worked as a trainer and coach for Microchip Technologies, a worldwide semiconductor company headquartered near Phoenix, Arizona, where I was living at the time. The company had risen from a struggling little enterprise into an international success with thousands of employees and soaring prosperity.

How did that remarkable reinvention happen? It was leadership. Creative, compassionate, courageously innovative leadership. It was offered by their CEO and Chairman Steve Sanghi, who chronicled the entire process of building the culture at Microchip in his provocative book, *Driving Excellence: How 'The Aggregate System' Turned Microchip Technology from a Failing Company to a Market Leader.*

I learned many positive lessons from working with leaders and managers inside that company. The one that stood out the most was their emphasis and commitment to systems. As the business sage G. Edwards Deming, pointed out long ago, "Every system is perfect for the result it is giving you." So, if you want a different result, change the system.

My cluttered office and chaotic system of scattering important books, papers, and sticky notes is perfect for the result it gives me. The impact of my approach was a lot of frustration and wasted time finding things when I needed them. It is a perfect system for that! If I wanted a result different and better than the frustration and time-wasting, I had to put in a different and better filing and organizing system.

That seems obvious and not that big of a game-changing idea. But it was huge for me because I would always *blame* myself or someone else when things went wrong. A messy office? I need psychotherapy! What's wrong with me?

And I saw that other people did that, too. A problem in the family? Find out who's to *blame* and have a confrontation. A problem in the company? Find out who's at fault! Put them on report or get rid of them immediately!

Because of my small victory in recognizing that I wasn't a flawed person for having paper chaos in my office, it resonated with me when I read what Steve Sanghi said about systems. He said, "… a focus on systems allows people (and companies) to solve their problems in a blameless way: If something goes wrong, it is no one's fault. We all pitch in to correct. The focus of the analysis postmortem is to find out what part of the system did not work, which process broke down, or what assumption went bad. The focus is not to find who to blame."[11]

---

[11] Phoenix Business Journal, 10Sept2013

Coaching clients away from personal blame

A client told me she wasn't doing a good job leading her weekly team meetings. She admitted showing up late sometimes, and rarely showing up prepared. She often thinks of important things to talk about to everyone while in a meeting, or even a day or two after it's over.

"What's wrong with me?" she asks. "Why am I so disorganized?"

In the past, I might have jumped right into exploring that question. I might have put on my amateur psychologist's cap and asked about her history, her childhood, or tried to unearth some subconscious reward she might be getting from being late and unprepared. Then, we'd try to find out what's wrong with her, personally, and see if there was a chance we could fix it.

But now, I invited her to look at her *system* for meeting preparation. The problem is her system for meeting preparation, not her psychological health. So first, we will explore how the current system is perfect for the result it's getting—her uneven performance in leading meetings. Then we'll look at what kind of system she could put in to get the result she wants. For example, before each meeting, she could set aside at least half an hour to create the agenda and make notes on what needs to be on it. And with that prep time, she'd never be scrambling around at the last minute, be unprepared, and show up late.

Don't take anything personally. Nothing others do is because of you. What others say and do is a projection of their own reality, their own dream. When you are immune to the opinions and actions of others, you won't be the victim of needless suffering."

~ Don Miguel Ruiz

I was recently coaching a leader writing a book. He was behind schedule and starting to ask, "What's wrong with me?" He wanted me to help determine if there were fatal weaknesses in his persona or character that led to procrastination.

I told him, "Let's not go into some illusory swamp where you personalize every issue and challenge and accept blame for them. Instead, let's elevate our exploration to focus on love, compassion, and your innate creativity. In other words, let's help you put in a new system that will lead to the book being written at a pace that the deadline for completion is easily met, and without blame (or shame) for any setbacks.

Changing our focus to systems

The great author and psychologist Dr. Nathaniel Branden is someone I learned from in-person, decades ago when he was my therapist, and from reading his insightful and bestselling books on consciousness, self-esteem, and taking responsibility. One simple story he told me about the effectiveness of taking a systems approach to problems, even in the personal world of home and family, really hit home.

Branden's wife complained about the stains from drops of coffee she'd find on the floor and carpet when she got up in the morning. Nathaniel would make his coffee in the kitchen in the morning and carry his brimming cup through the living room into his office to start his day's work. And later, his wife would inevitably find spots on the floor.

He would apologize and try to be more mindful, but the spots would start appearing again after a time. It was a problem. And he was to blame, right? What was wrong with him? Didn't he care about how the home looked? Was he assuming that it was her job to clean up after him? Like most even minor problems, they descend into criticism and blame when people are involved.

But Nathaniel was gifted and practiced maintaining his self-esteem and not taking things personally. So, he created a new system for transporting coffee from the kitchen to his office. Rather than filling the cup to the brim, his new system was to fill his cup two-thirds full.

Then, when he carried the cup, the coffee would stay inside. From that day on, there was no spillage, ever.

For me, this story hit home. It was not as "big" a problem as those that leaders and coaches confront in this ever-changing, high-tech, hyper-connected world, but it made the point for me. Filling the coffee cup full up and trying not to spill was his previous system, and it was perfect for the result he was getting: spots on the carpet. Filling it two-thirds full was the new system that had become perfect for the new result—coffee in his office with no trail of spots. And no contention with his wife over this now non-issue.

Our brave new world

As highlighted by Will's previous chapters, the brave new world that leaders work in today requires leadership willing to shift and share power to bring the whole team of players into the process. That creates trust and collaboration and builds a flexible team of creators. Conversely, it doesn't work to respond to changing world winds with a brittle, old-school hierarchy led by commanders expecting mindless obedience.

My work as a coach is to help a leader of today see that power-sharing is not power lost. As Microchip Technology's incredible global success demonstrates, a deliberately-created, systems-focused culture leads to more extraordinary achievement, not less.

We have seen the descent into chaos and despair when

political and governmental leaders communicate by personal attacks on the people who disagree with them. Suggesting a better way of governing to such "leaders" is met with a personal attack on the person doing the suggesting or the questioning. Ad hominem becomes ad nauseam, and soon the average person doesn't even want to watch or read the daily news.

And when political parties (of all philosophies) are putting up "electable" but ill-qualified, curmudgeonly candidates for office who have no talent for leadership, we see the painfully embarrassing and costly results of such a system.

Microcosms of that chaos occur in families, small businesses, and educational organizations, and everywhere good and true leadership is absent.

We now have the opportunity to wake up to support each other in collaborative creation and create blameless systems that depersonalize the outcomes.

This shift needs to happen now—and it can.

Eleven

Fear Less, Leader

Will

In my first executive role I was the epitome of wet behind the ears. But I had degrees in finance and law and wore a suit, white shirt, and tie every day to work. Each day I thought to myself, "Put me in coach. I'm ready!"

One day, the "coach" (my boss) arrived in my office with a directive. "You need to terminate the Director of Human Resources by this Friday." In no time, my head was spinning with the reality of how much "executive experience" I had: none. I had never fired anyone. I had no idea how to go about it, and my CEO thought it was time to figure it out for myself. I felt afraid to ask him for help.

The man who needed to go was twenty years older than me and had a wife and a couple of kids. I spent the next few days contending with questions like: "How will he care for his family? Will he lose his house because he can't make the payments? How will he react? What if he gets angry and says, 'You can't fire the Director of HR!'—or worse, 'You're just an errand boy; I want to speak to the CEO.'"

And that was just the anxiety part.

"What's wrong with me?"

I also felt palpable fear. Fear that I wasn't competent, fear of failing at the task at hand, fear that I would never be the executive I had dreamed about, and fear that I would be fired for bungling the first opportunity I'd had to prove my worth.

The day arrived, and my tie felt extra tight around my neck. I had written notes with answers to every question I thought might come up. I put my suit jacket on, buttoned it, and walked into his office. I had the first sentence I planned to say written down, but it was hard to read because my hand was shaking. "Mark, I am very sorry to tell you that your work here is done. You are being terminated."

Fortunately for me, Mark said, "Yeah, my head hasn't really been in this for a while. I was wondering when I was going to get a visit." And he sheepishly smiled at me.

In my naivete, I hadn't even considered that he might be expecting it and be relieved. I was a little angry with him because of my energy spent on being ready for what turned out to be a "non-event," but the real battle had been inside me. I feared confronting this man who hadn't been giving fair value to the organization for a long time and knew it. How could I possibly be a leader if I felt fear over handling this situation?

After decades of leadership experience, I can report that the "fearless leader" is a myth. In fact, it's worse than a myth. It's a lie. To one degree or another, fear is in the shadow of every leader, both in times of challenge and of smooth sailing.

Coping with "the voice"

When you accept leadership responsibility, you will have greeted yet another voice in your head—the one representing everything that could go wrong under your guidance and direction. It is a loud and persistent voice both for new leaders and for those forced out of their comfort zones. It is perfectly capable of overwhelming the judgment that had served you so well in other contexts.

The voice speaks not only about what could go wrong—it also says things like, "You don't even know where to start." "Even if you did, why would people listen to you?" "The people on the team know more about what needs to be done than you do." "What made you think you could do this? Were you out of your mind?"

The same persistently aggravating voice will also challenge you when things are going right, "You've made it through the first year, but the organization is bigger now and you've never led anything this complicated." "You made a great hire, but she has much better communication skills than you. You screwed up again; she is a threat." "Even if you make it through another year, you won't be able to sustain it long enough to get your kids through college."

This isn't a productive conversation (nor a conversation at all). It is fear showing up as an unwelcome interrogator peeling back the façade of your leader persona and exposing your shortcomings. Giving in to this voice for too long can sustain fear, uncertainty, and doubt and keep you from making timely and balanced judgments.

One of the best ways to quiet this disabling narrative is to move into action. If you are making decisions and taking action, your focus will shift away from what the voice has to say.

Like so many old-school leaders at the time, I developed my coping skills mainly through trial and error. I was never comfortable discussing my battles with fear with those close enough to me to have insight into them. Those people would, I thought, see me as a fallible human being! It was a case of being fearful of the consequences of talking about fear—a shadow of a shadow.

As I have described, eventually, the catalog of "what I knew" began to override fear in many situations. But the higher the stakes and complexity—the more at risk I feel—I could (and still can) count on fear to show itself, ready for a fight.

I learned from experience that leadership is not about eliminating fear but transcending it. In all its forms, colors, masks, mysteries, and seeming complexity, fear is like fuel to a forest fire. It becomes the sucker of oxygen, the drainer of creativity, the darkness turning you inward. It drives you to protectionism, isolation, lashing out, numbing, foreboding of failure, and even fear of fear.

Enormous energy can be turned toward action when we question the apparent "facts" underlying our fear and the low probability of the adverse outcomes we are "certain" will come.

Twelve

Replacing Fear with Curiosity

Steve

Before going into training and coaching, I was a disaster as a leader. I ran two different advertising agencies into ruin and bankruptcy. This was all from (in retrospect) being ignorant about the importance of leading with honesty, accountability, and compassion. Like Will, I led from fear and what I thought was self-preservation. As painful as those days were for me (and those I "led"), there was deep, hard-won learning.

No labels, no judgment

I first became aware of the true power of coaching years ago when I hired my coach, Steve Hardison. When I first met with him and told him my history of failure, he helped me transform the shame and guilt of those memories into learning experiences designed for my improvement and upliftment.

It took a while, and I got a lot of help from him, but I finally learned to shift my focus to who my client was *being*, not just what they were *doing*.

At first, I didn't understand that logic. My fearful, vulnerable, cowardly self felt like who I *actually was*. How could that possibly be changed? But my coach helped me see that what I felt was my permanent identity was merely a story I'd long believed in. What if I could internalize that who I was *being* today was based on stories that I'd been telling myself since childhood? And what if those stories could be seen for what they were, and just dropped? Could I then create and show up as who I wanted to be?

Had I been receiving that level of coaching back in my unsuccessful ad agency days, both of those companies would have thrived. The talent was there. The people I brought onto the team were great at what they did. The only thing missing was leadership. I was the head of the company, and the company was rotting from the head down.

It's what occurred," my coach would say. "It's not who you are. Who you are is yours to create from this moment on."

In my early years of working with him, I wanted the same coaching sought by many of the leaders I work with today. I wanted to be coached at the level of tactics, strategies, and action steps. I wanted him to *tell me* what to do so that I could turn my disastrous life around. But I soon learned from him that impactful coaching goes deeper than that.

Before I had fully internalized what he was trying to show me, I thought my value in coaching leaders was in what I wanted for myself—offering prescriptive and directive "what to do" instructions. It was somewhat akin to what Will described as "old-school" leadership but applied to coaching. And I thought doing it that way proved how smart and valuable I was to my clients.

I gave lots of advice on what to say, how to say it, what to do, and how to do it, and then I'd schedule my client to come back to me to review what happened. I was coaching their situation and focusing on the specific solution that seemed required from my perspective.

But this kind of coaching was shallow and temporary. There were often some good outer-world results, but nothing was changing at a deeper level inside the client. They were not becoming more independent and autonomous due to being lifted up by me.

Limiting beliefs

I finally, really, discovered what my coach was trying to get across to me; great coaching begins with the client opening up to the possibility of inner transformation. The outer world of circumstance and relationships will change for the better soon enough if attention is paid first to who the client is being, not just the (sometimes dysfunctional) things they are doing.

This "opening up" approach became critically important when I was later coaching leaders. My work improved and was more impactful when I paid more attention to the leader as a whole person—body, mind, and spirit—with fears and feelings.

As Will's life and story as a leader illustrate, people are not stuck with the negative and limiting labels they've given themselves. I learned that the value-added work of a coach is to help their client let those labels fall away so that they can create the future from a clean slate.Effective coaching is a collaborative effort, not (as many newer coaches mistakenly try to pull off) a superior person attempting to correct an inferior person.

I've learned to share my past weaknesses and failures with clients, just as my coach has always done with me. It creates immediate relatedness and a context of non-judgment from which we can truly create together. Disclosing my fallibility is almost always a great ice-breaker.

I was recently working with the young leader of a company on uncovering some of the limiting beliefs he had buried inside himself. Accepting those limitations had him creating unnecessary communication and relationship issues in his company. He always thought he was "hard-wired" and had to change the people around him because there was no way he would be able to change himself.

As modern studies in neuroscience have proven, though, even the brain itself can change in dramatic ways when new habits (and the resultant new neural pathways) are deliberately developed. Fortunately, the work this young leader and I are doing together is beginning to show him how infinite his capacity for change is.

Primarily at the level of who he is being for his people at work, and even his family at home.

An old-world, egocentric leader who's labeled herself or himself a permanent and inherent "introvert" or even, as was the case of the great Werner Erhard, an "asshole" (self-describing his early days), has the power to change. Forgive me, but that's exciting!

Fear of coaching leaders

My friend and colleague Devon Bandison coaches people from high-level athletes, to people who want to be better parents, to organizational leaders. He coaches them all the same way, and his book, *Fatherhood Is Leadership*, is a classic in the fields of parenting and leadership and a very worthwhile read.

Devon says, "Fathers today are more involved than ever. Changing diapers, playing ball, helping with homework, and the crises and joys of childhood, adolescence, and beyond. And the time we spend nurturing our children has a tremendous influence on their lives. Children with active fathers are happier, get better grades, and make better choices."

Of course, that goes for mothers, teachers, and people in all roles of life. In truth, leaders aren't just the heads of organizations. It would be hard to find anyone who does not have some leadership opportunities and roles in their lives.

Therefore, great coaches like Devon Bandison don't have to specialize in coaching leaders to be good at it. The principle of helping people discover *who they can be* is the same no matter the labels.

Many coaches I know (including me early in my career) are totally intimidated by the thought of coaching a leader in an organization. They fear that they don't know enough about business to do a credible job.

But what they realize (and I eventually did too) is that a leader in business has the same internal fears and insecurities that anyone else has. Often even more so, being overly self-conscious about people looking up to them and expecting to find a "fearless leader" who always has their act together.

Often that level of fear and self-consciousness leads to exaggerated expressions of ego and domination, then to multiple communication and relationship problems in the organization. (We see this kind of bloviating ego exaggeration in many of our political leaders today.)

Sometimes this "imposter" fear will have a leader go in the other direction: hiding out, not sharing vital information, and finding imaginary "power" in keeping secrets and not being accessible to their people.

In either of those two leadership malfunctions, the opportunity for the coaching work is to help the leader identify the ego-centric, fear-based belief systems that keep them stuck.

Seeing the disempowering belief for what it is enables the client to experience new pathways of freedom, compassion, and creativity in their professional (and personal) lives.

Radical accountability erases fear

Teams that care about and understand each other better work better together. But people today enter an organization from cultures and personal histories of vast diversity. To an enlightened, compassionate leader, this situation can create a rich and adventurous opportunity for creative team-building. Leaders can see an opportunity to provide their people a fresh sense of belonging in the context of the organizational culture as a "living" place.

But the keyword is "enlightened." The leader must be enlightened about their responsibility to lead the way with a commitment to create that culture as a daily reality, not just a "value" mentioned only at the yearly company retreat.

The leaders I have coached have had a wide variety of awareness about their responsibility in that area. Sometimes, in my less graceful and compassionate days as a coach, I would share with an ineffective leader my (perhaps too-descriptive) metaphor, "A fish rots from the head down."

After they'd grasped it, I'd follow up with what they probably took as another challenge to their ego: "If there's a problem, you're the problem." You will create the culture and morale of your team in the positive direction you want it to go, or it may default and descend into attitudinal anarchy and absence of loyalty and trust."

But a coach's job is to help convert the leader's wounded ego (and urge to get defensive) into a positive sense of new opportunity. Once I reminded a leader or manager that if there was a morale and dependability "problem" then *they* were the problem, I'd quickly follow with, "But that's the good news."

"Why is my being the problem good news?" they would ask.

"Because if you're the problem, you're also the solution."

That's when our real work would start. Exploring options about what they needed to **do** to change morale, culture, and team cohesion for the better, but even more important, who they needed to **be** that would model and encourage the spirit they wanted to create.

Coaching sessions for leaders are at their best when they offer a place where fears and self-doubt can be safely revealed. A place where the leader can show up as a "whole person" and take off their armor.

Thirteen

Leadership is Listening for Understanding

Will

I have been directive as a communicator for much of my life, as those who know me well will attest. I have been so concerned with getting into action that while listening to a team member, colleague, or collaborator, I have often already started moving toward a solution when I think, "I've got it."

Yet there can be several issues with this approach: I may not "get it" as much as I think I have—or at all. A deeper explanation or analysis may be valuable. An immediate or close-in solution may not actually lead to an optimal outcome. Errors might occur that could have been avoided if I had taken a pause for both listening and reflection.

I certainly missed opportunities to teach and mentor others in the complete inquiry, analysis, and decision-making process. My providing such leadership could have been much more impactful than the speed with which a resolution might have been achieved. As the saying goes, "If you give a man a fish, he will eat for a day; if you teach him to fish, he will eat for a lifetime."

My approach also could be intimidating, leading to shutting down people with specialized knowledge, who might have offered more had I allowed them to contribute. I know for my own part that whenever someone over-speaks or cuts me off—as I have been known to do to others—I am much less likely to stay engaged.

My failure to rein in my desire for rapid change assured for years that my then-inferior listening skills would stay stuck where they were. Fortunately, with the help of my coach, Steve Chandler, I found enlightenment—at least in the art of listening.

"Tell me about yourself."

How does a leader who hasn't embraced mindfulness, empathy, and collaboration take a step in that direction? An excellent place to start is by viewing every conversation as an opportunity for listening in a new way—with an elevated sense of attention and curiosity and awareness of the emotions being expressed, in addition to the content.

Given the numbing effect of the information overload of our times, being fully present as a listener is a tall order. But for leaders with the desire to show up as mindful, empathetic, and collaborative, there can be a significant return on the time and attention invested as more engaged listeners.

As a powerful tool in communication, listening

leverages the ego. Researchers from the Harvard University Social Cognitive and Affective Neuroscience Lab utilized functional magnetic resonance imaging for clues as to why this is the case. They found, "On average, people spend 60 percent of conversations talking about themselves. This figure jumps to 80 percent when communicating via social media platforms . . . Why, in a world full of ideas to discover, develop, and discuss, do people prefer to spend a majority of their time talking and have it be about them?"[12]

Because it feels good. "Self-disclosure, like other more traditionally recognized stimuli, may be inherently pleasurable—and that people may be motivated to talk about themselves more than other topics (no matter how interesting or important these non-self-oriented topics may be)."

Keeping in mind that we tap into other people's good feelings when we give them space to discuss themselves is sometimes hard to do. After all, we, too, get pleasure from talking about ourselves.

To set the table for listening, you must signal that that is your role. You can make clear through your actions that the speaker is getting your undivided attention. Turn off your phone and remove it from view. Sit up and make an effort to appear pleasant and open. Be prepared to take notes. Remind yourself not to interrupt, and don't be too

---

[12] https://www.scientificamerican.com/article/the-neuroscience-of-everybody-favorite-topic-themselves/

quick to fill any silence. Try to resist saying, "I'm just here to listen."

Open the door

Be prepared to "prime the pump" by having open-ended questions at the ready. These are questions that create space for expansive responses. Such questions invite the other person to jump in or keep going. Often they may start with "how" or "what." These are questions that cannot be fully answered with the words "yes" or "no," nor with another kind of short, complete, unambiguous answer ("What would you like for lunch?" "Pastrami on rye with spicy brown mustard, hold the pickle").

Some examples of open-ended questions include, "How are you feeling about your new role?" "What could I do to better support you in pursuing a greater sense of overall well-being?" "What are some skills you would like to gain or improve over the next twenty-four months?" Prepare a germane follow-up question or two to encourage the speaker to continue in their role.

Ending the conversation with a recap— "Here's what we discussed …"—and clarifying any next steps, is an indication of a complete communication.

The most difficult challenge for me in this evolution toward "leadership listening" has been slowing down. It takes time and patience to allow the communication to unfold. This approach will rarely feel efficient for someone with many competing demands—most leaders.

This listening time, you might be thinking, could be used for your "own work." You may sometimes conclude, "This person is talking about wacky [or inappropriate, or only self-serving] things." But in the long run this deeper listening will serve the organization and its people well. Which means the leader is truly serving through listening *and* hearing.

Just as we discussed that there is a time and place for leaders owning decisions, this is also true in managing communication. Given the multiplicity of leadership's responsibilities and priorities, a leader must create and enforce boundaries in many conversations. This of course depends on context—namely the person, subject, relevance, and timing of the conversation. Even when something needs to be said and heard, the leader and team members must understand time, place, and priorities. It is up to the leader to convey this in a way that continues to promote listening as the often-better part of communication.

Obviously, culture change is a process that cannot be permitted to threaten the survivability and success of the organization. But, as with most things in leadership—it's a balancing act. The organization's purpose must be served through thick and thin. If not, the opportunities for listening and hearing the team members will simply evaporate as a result of the decline and fall of the organization.

From time to time, test yourself. Do you notice that your curiosity has deepened, your listening is more powerful, and that people *want* you to hear them? Have you also practiced getting across that sometimes "now" is not a good time for you to be able to listen and hear as you would like? Leadership requires both.

Fourteen

Too Much Focus on "What Should I Say?"

Steve

I used to think listening was not a creative act. I viewed listening as what I had to endure until it was my turn to talk. I used to think talking and communicating brilliant ideas and advice was what coaching was all about. I was just like the leaders I coach, who believe that leading is all about telling people what they should do, and who do most of the talking in one-to-one and team meetings.

But both the leaders and I were incomplete in our work. We were short-changing the possibility of being better at our jobs.

I have learned a great deal from the wisdom of a teacher and author named Brenda Ueland. She delivers marvelous instruction about creative writing and even more so about life itself. One of her most emphatic teachings is about the underrated power of listening. Here's what she had to say about listening, and it's not an exaggeration to say that this single, diamond-sharp observation changed my life: "When we are listened to, it creates us, makes us unfold and expand. Ideas begin to grow within us and come to life."

With this insight, I looked for opportunities to listen more and better. And the more I did that, the more insights and breakthroughs occurred for my clients. Becoming a better listener also changed my relationships with my wife, children, and friends.

When we are listened to, it creates us, makes us unfold and expand. Ideas begin to grow within us and come to life.

~ Brenda Ueland

It later hit me that what's good for the coach is also good for the client, especially when they want to improve in leading their organizations.

When the leaders I coach have problems with their partners or direct reports or customers and clients or family members at home, they usually want me to help them find the right thing to *say*. Many questions in a coaching session would have the leader asking, "What should I say when . . . ?" Or "How do I talk to her about . . . ?" Or "What do you think I should tell my team about . . . ?"

Often, I recommend to them that they do a listening

session. Just meet with the person and find out what they're thinking. See what you can learn. If you really want to improve your relationship with someone in the organization, allow them to *be* and *feel* heard and understood.

"No agenda" listening

Parenting is clearly a form of leadership, often the most challenging of all! In my younger years, I was a single father raising four children on my own and making a real mess of the whole thing. The more adventurous my kids were in exploring problematic modes of behavior, the more I talked, taught, and reprimanded them—always judging and correcting.

Fortunately, I was desperate enough to seek help, and a brilliant family counselor showed me a new approach I would never have thought to take. When one of my daughters was having a particularly rebellious phase at home and school, my counselor gave me what I thought was a weird assignment.

"The next time you are with her," she said, "see if you can be there with no agenda."

I realized how unusual that sounded to me. I had to confess to the counselor that I couldn't remember any conversations with my daughter where I didn't have an agenda. I was always talking, thinking I needed to guide and correct her. I was advising her on better ways to think and act. Always. No matter what my daughter said to me,

I'd come back with a correction or direction on how to improve, from my perspective only, what she was doing.

My experiments with sitting with my daughter with no agenda, with me just listening, were met with suspicion at the start. She'd say, "Okay, Dad, give it to me. What are you waiting to tell me that you want me to do?"

But over time, our relationship got better and better, and her behavioral challenges started to go away.

Although this is a personal parenting anecdote, it is here to simplify and emphasize the hidden power of listening. My relationship with my daughter improved, and her actions in life became more positive because I had no agenda. I did nothing.

But it wasn't actually "nothing." On the contrary, it was deceptively and surprisingly powerful.

My counselor coached me to listen. And I later found that when I encouraged the leaders I coach to experiment with and practice more listening, the positive results would reinforce its value.

Letting coaching and leadership combine

Will Keiper's leader's sections of this book are wake-up calls to the urgency of more innovative, compassionate, and courageous leadership in the face of rapid change and rising personal insecurity in the workplace. The quickest undoing of a leader today is insufficiency in listening. Their people are more concerned about feeling connected, appreciated, and holistically fulfilled in their work-life endeavors. They can't get to these positive feelings when their leader doesn't listen to and *hear* them.

In static, hierarchical management (when it was the norm), a leader could get away with dominating, outbound communication. So people were accustomed to having their activities micro-managed in a one-sided way.

But leaders today need to mix some life-coaching and relationship skills into their personal operating systems for their team members to succeed and grow and flow with the times.

As a coach of today's leaders, my mission is to help my clients see that skill deficits in these areas are not a result of hardwired character flaws or seemingly permanent personality traits. Breakthroughs in modern neuroscience (that confirm long-standing spiritual principles and meditative traditions) prove that the brain is more adaptive at any age than we ever thought was possible.

People who think they are "not a good listener," "not that good with people," or "lack compassion for others" can learn through patient coaching that those are mere lines of development that have not yet been sufficiently explored and cultivated.

Fifteen

There Are No Wrong Notes

Will

During a 1960s concert in Stuttgart, Germany, jazz pianist Herbie Hancock played an unintended and, he thought, very pronounced wrong chord. Bandleader and trumpeter Miles Davis responded with a series of notes that made Hancock's chord sound intentional. Hancock later said of the moment: "He did what any jazz musician should always try to do, and that is to make anything that happens into something of value."

Davis had immediately improvised, moving into the next riff using the "wrong" chord as his jumping-off point. He didn't miss a beat. He was focused on the task at hand—completing a professional performance for a paying and discerning audience. Afterward, you would've been far more likely to hear from the patrons, "Wow, that was an amazing experience!" instead of "Ouch, I can still hear Herbie's foul chord ringing in my ear; what a disappointing performance."

Improvise, adapt, overcome

Improvisation, in general terms, is ". . . a spontaneous behavior (collectively or individually), and therefore dependent on team members' attitudes, experience, motivation, intuition, and individual skills."[13] A leader and a team more skilled at improvisation will have a performance advantage in almost any dynamic environment.

The ethos of the U.S. Marines and most Special Forces organizations worldwide is "Improvise. Adapt. Overcome." There may not be a single advantage in many serious situations other than acting immediately with what you have at hand. The resources are the resources, ample or scarce. Given what you have to work with, creativity, speed and urgency matter more than anything else.

Applying this in a leadership situation could mean acknowledging what happened and immediately engaging the team in developing options for creating a path forward with the resources at hand. Good leaders and team members will not need to attach an emotional label to the situation such as, "It's bad," or "It's wrong." In my work with companies and leaders, I suggest teaching the other leaders and team members to simply report the facts of "what happened" and not sensationalize the situation.

In an article in The MIT Sloan Management Review entitled, "Learning the Art of Business Improvisation," the core skills were identified as ". . . problem-solving, communication and expression, proper use of language,

---

[13] https://sloanreview.mit.edu/article/learning-the-art-of-business-improvisation/

creativity, and visualization abilities."

In the study that underpinned it, the researchers—who focused on the dynamics of software project management teams—asked, "Can the improvisation capabilities of the team be enhanced so that it is better able to more creatively adapt to unexpected changes ... and turn a challenge into a source of competitive advantage?" They found that focused effort in three areas can help develop these improvisation competencies.

Build a culture that recognizes and views changes positively. Greater levels of improvisation came from teams that displayed a positive attitude toward dealing with and accepting ambiguity and project changes... The focus should be on helping teams anticipate and recognize changing circumstances and make more rapid and accurate decisions.

Create the right team structure and environment. Project teams with greater improvisation [abilities] had more frequent meetings and interactions ... The meetings allowed more frequent face-to-face interactions focused on the project and improved communication quality. That, in turn, enabled teams to respond more quickly to changes.

Provide management practices and tools that facilitate improvisation. Teams with greater improvisation characteristics were more likely to use agile management approaches, techniques, and tools. In fact, teams that embraced an agile approach were nine times more likely to have high levels of improvisation compared with teams that used a more traditional . . . approach.[14]

It makes perfect sense that improvisational skills could significantly impact an organization's adaptability in rapidly shifting dynamics. Moreover, such skills can be taught and learned in organizations, just as in the worlds of special military ops and jazz (where they are a foundational musical requirement).

In the case of an organization, awareness of required changes will often first arise at the level of the person accountable for specific "subsystems" rather than the leadership level. Having a system that allows those key individuals to make the immediate, necessary adjustments will serve as a "first response." This system will, of course, require a plan, a cultural shift, experimentation, and readiness ahead of the moment when improvisation is needed.

"Why are we doing this?"

During many business planning sessions that I led or participated in as CEO, president, board member, or facilitator, I would frequently ask about something previously decided, "Remind me again, why are we doing this?" The response would often be, "I thought we already made this decision weeks ago." I answered, "We did, but can you explain it to me again? We decided with

---

[14] https://sloanreview.mit.edu/article/learning-the-art-of-business-improvisation/ A reprint can be purchased at http://mitsmr.com/1SPz5DJ

the information available at the time. Let's make sure that the reasons for the initial decision are still valid given what we have learned since then."

If the decision is still sound, you can affirm what supports it. If the decision needs adjustment, this question will open the door to the required conversation.

There is surely nothing quite so useless as doing with great efficiency what should not be done at all.

~ Peter Drucker

The sooner you know that something once important is no longer relevant or needs to be rethought, the sooner you can make adjustments or abandon it.

The question, "Why are we doing this?" and what flows from asking it, support good decision-making for a company and good mental health for those spending time doing things that have outlived their relevancy. In addition, asking this question will build a culture that welcomes challenges to the status quo.

Here is a simple mantra for this process:

Gather information. Evaluate. Decide.

Gather information. Evaluate. Make adjustments.

Gather information. Evaluate. Make adjustments.

Repeat continuously.

Make it your own. Give it a name. Invite your team to modify it for application in your organization. Tag decisions that can benefit from this continuous improvement process and calendar regular follow-ups.

You will have reprocessed the original decision in making a timely correction or adaptation. No matter how good at the time, an initial decision becomes a prospect for improvement.

This approach permits the application of new knowledge from all sources, including the results-to-date of the previous decision. This process supports rapid adaptation in dynamic environments.[15] And it opens the door for greater improvisation because the more the dynamics are understood and responses practiced, the greater your facility with them will be when they shift. Just like jazz.

If the adaptive decision improves the outcome by

---

[15] My first notice of this concept came from learning about the OODA Loop, a cycle of: observe–orient–decide–act. It is credited to military strategist and United States Air Force Colonel John Boyd. Boyd applied the concept to air combat operations, sometimes called aerial "dogfights." Failure to rapidly adapt based upon new information could be fatal in those situations.

five—or even one—percent, the organization will very likely outperform others over time. An even better case is that the original decision is fully validated—proof that the team and the leadership are succeeding in decision-making and execution.

Sixteen

Brainstorming Versus Problem-Solving

Steve

I noticed that a CEO I was coaching was frequently operating from a negative mindset and communicated that way. He was the epitome of an old-style boss: harsh, no-nonsense, and authoritarian. He kept saying, "It's their issue if they can't deal with the truth. If there's a problem, I call it a problem." He had a hard time believing there was value in a different approach to communicating with his team.

So as an experiment to show him what I was trying to get him to see, I asked him to schedule a meeting with forty of his top people from all departments and book two conference rooms for a two-hour workshop.

"Why two conference rooms?" he said. "We can fit them in one."

I told him I wanted them evenly but randomly separated into two rooms. I wanted them to work on what most of the company, especially my client, kept referring to as "the problem with the warehouse."

The problem with the warehouse, to over-simplify it, was that the dispatcher (and they'd tried several people in that position) would eventually be in constant conflict with the service team on the matter of acquiring and distributing parts for the service team to use in the field.

The service team complained that the warehouse didn't respect their needs and requests, especially the time-sensitive ones. And the warehouse complained that the service team didn't appreciate the limitations and constraints of the warehouse and that they kept making unreasonable requests.

The CEO, and the managers of both departments, had tried all kinds of solutions to this ongoing problem and none were lasting. As a result, the morale of each team was low, and each group blamed the other.

When the day came, and the people were divided and sent into two separate conference rooms across the hall, I went to the front of the first room, where the people were sitting around a large table. The CEO was there to observe. I had a moment of fear that my language and communication experiment might not work, but it was too late to back out.

I told the people in that room that they'd been gathered to work on the warehouse problem and see if, by working together, they could solve it. I saw a lot of eye-rolling and heard some groans, so I asked what the matter was.

"We've been trying to solve this problem for years now," one woman said. Another man added, "If it hasn't been resolved after years of trying, how will two more hours help anything?"

I acknowledged the truth of what they were saying and how understandable their feelings might be, but I wanted a show of hands of who would still be willing to try. And I think it was because the CEO was standing in the back of the room that they all eventually raised their hands.

"Good!" I said. "I admire you for being willing to try. We'll come back at the end of your time together to see how you did."

The CEO and I walked across the hall to the other group, and he was not looking optimistic. I stood up front and the CEO, once again, took his place in the back. Another flurry of anxiety passed through me as I realized that this might be my last day working with him

I explained to the people in this room that I used to work with an ad agency, and that the creative department often scheduled a brainstorming session to come up with ideas to present to an account we were pitching. I asked if they knew what a brainstorming session was, and some did but most didn't.

"It's designed to be loose and fun," I said. "This will be all about the situation at the warehouse that is not currently working. One of you will stand at the whiteboard, and you'll keep going around the room suggesting ideas that will be written on the board. The ideas can be as crazy and weird as you want; say what comes to mind. Some of your ideas will feel stupid, and some won't—but it doesn't matter."

"As you go along, you'll treat all ideas the same, and at the end, you'll look at the board and vote on the three ideas you think have the best chance of working, and then you'll rank them in order of potential. The only rule is that you keep it fun and light-hearted and not worry about any kind of outcome." I left out the characterization of the situation as a "longstanding problem." The CEO didn't notice this difference from the set-up for the first group.

They got the assignment, and the CEO and I left the room and went into his office so that I could explain what I wanted him to see. My message to him was that heavy-handed, fear-based language and communication would always result in fewer effective solutions created by his people. I told him that continuously framing the warehouse situation as a "serious problem that needed to be solved" would keep it in that worrisome category. He was still skeptical.

"What's going on in there?"

After the first hour, I wanted to do a listening check outside the doors, so he and I walked the long corridor back to the conference rooms. At the serious, problem-solving group's door, we could barely hear what was being said. Their voices were low and lacked any animation.

The other room was completely different. Outside their door we heard laughter and loud voices. "What's going on in there?" my CEO said.

"Brainstorming," I said. "It's fun. And notice that when I set it up, I made no mention of a problem."

"But the warehouse thing *is* a problem," he said.

"That's been your choice of label," I said. "Words matter."

At the end of the two hours, we went to the first room, and I asked if they'd been able to come up with a solution to the warehouse problem. They hit me with all kinds of reasons why not. "We've already tried everything." The service people in the room told me there would be no solution until the warehouse changed its ways, and the warehouse people said the opposite was true.

When we went to the other room, the group looked upbeat and excited. Then, the brainstorm leader said, "We first laughed at the idea we now think is the best one."

"One of the people from service suggested that if the dispatcher at the warehouse were from the service department, it would solve it. We thought the warehouse people would object, but they said, 'Are you kidding? We'd love that. Our dispatchers go through hell trying to understand the service department's needs. If we had one of them in our building doing the dispatching, we could work with them all day to know how to make our acquisitions in a way that makes it work for everyone.'"

The company put that system in place right away, and it worked—if not perfectly—far better than the previous system, and both departments had a noticeable improvement in morale. The animosity they'd had for each other began to fade away. With the service person doing the dispatch job from the warehouse, the two departments were in positive communication all day long.

Proving the benefits of converting the company's "problems" into creative projects and opportunities for change was the beginning of a great relationship I had coaching that CEO from then on. He realized that as the leader, he *set the context* for every challenge that arose. He also learned that his *words matter* in doing so.

Seventeen

Collaborative Creation

Will

Steve Chandler and I have had a leader-coach relationship for more than ten years. We brought into that relationship our work experience with for-profit and other organizations of all shapes and sizes in many locations worldwide. We served as entrepreneurs, executives, board members, investors, consultants, mentors, trainers, and coaches.

Initially, Steve didn't have to say much. He couldn't. I didn't stop talking about what I thought I knew about the challenges I was facing and what to do about them. Even if he had wanted to (and that is why he was there—and I was paying him), he couldn't weigh in until I left the building. I had forgotten to both ask questions *and* listen.

Fortunately, that situation didn't last too long.

He later wrote, "When I first met Will Keiper, I thought he had a bit of a problem. He wasn't a very good compromiser. His preference was to challenge 'go-along-to-get-along' company cultures and people. He was a man on the move, and he sometimes came off as impatient. Some called him 'brutally honest,' with the emphasis on 'brutal.' He would call it getting to the 'obvious truth.'"

I thought this description of me was a little extreme, but by that time, I was listening.

Since then, we developed a foundation and rhythm for "how to show up in the world" that has changed my life. He helped me move from "challenger" towards "listener" and "seeker" of the opinions of others. From a directive to a much more collaborative leader.

Leadership coaches who succeed in developing enlightened leaders, including Steve, learn that the process is one of collaborative creation ("co-creation"). Their shared interest and objectives are developing the leadership and coaching skills required for the leader to create an open, resilient, and adaptable culture. They work together to *create*, not *solve*.

In my case, I didn't expect Steve to supply me with expert solutions to my specific challenges. The issues we address, whether it is my business consulting, professional coaching, or writing, are framed in, "What could we create to address this challenge? Where is the opportunity in it? Who would you need to 'be' (present yourself as) to do what is required?"

I then go off to do the solving, the leading, and the writing, harnessing and building on the creative energy we initiated together.

Casualty

As we've attempted to make clear throughout this book, we believe that leadership in the 21st century is all about building an organizational culture that will be capable of rapid transformation. I have firsthand experience of how impossible it is to do this alone.

Several years ago, I ran a global business for the first time. It was a publicly-owned company that required restructuring, including significant consolidation and downsizing. We had software and hardware development occurring in six countries, and eight administrative offices in multiple regions of the world. We distributed our products in over 100 countries. I was a highly experienced executive and game for the challenge but painfully aware of the differences in managing in an international environment.

Fear remained my old, reliable companion, and I was dealing with acres of the flotsam and jetsam from decades of the foibles of "previous management." I needed a trusted, independent sounding board more than ever. Rather than working with an objective outside advisor, I trusted certain board members for advice and counsel. Unfortunately (and understandably), they had their own fears, demons, and agendas, that were obvious and, in some cases, destructive. In other words, they were fallible human beings, and it didn't feel as though they had my back.

They didn't have coaching or mentoring experience to

guide and support me. And at the time, I lacked the objectivity and patience to navigate the enormous tasks at hand *and* take the time to listen and engage with them in a productive, patient, and collegial way.

Over two years, my team and I successfully restructured the business. About two years thereafter, the company was merged into a competitor for over seven times the company's market value when I stepped in as CEO.

For many reasons, I wasn't there for the victory lap. If I had taken the time to engage with a trusted coach as an ally, rather than taking out my frustrations directly with the people who were my "bosses," there is no doubt I would have been. But I lost sight of the fact that managing the board's expectations was simply a part of overall leadership (something I knew and of which any skillful coach would have regularly reminded me—and probably told me to quit whining).

This conflict led to me being a casualty of a hard-fought battle to raise the value of the business. We agreed to a mutual parting of our ways at the end of the first two years, and I left the company to "pursue other opportunities." The choice to not have a coach in my corner cost me several million dollars and a few years of regret for losing perspective.

The value of collaborative creation

I believe that each leader should have a trusted

listener, truth-teller, and guide outside the organization they lead. For a leader aspiring to be their best—this kind of resource—is a requirement, not a luxury.

The best leadership and coaching are based on thoughtful, clear, compassionate communication, including deep listening. These skills improve with greater awareness and practice and have long been the foundation for successful coaching.

Leaders who succeed at transforming the culture in their organizations know that the process will be one of co-creation between the leader and the individual team members and among the team members. Today's leadership imperative is developing a resilient, continuously improving organization, ready and capable of rapid adaptation when required. For leaders to accomplish this, enhancing their coaching skills is an essential part of a "kinder, gentler" but highly productive creative process among collaborators.

Eighteen

You Don't Have to Have All the Answers

Steve

As we talked about her difficulties leading a team of major gift fundraisers, my client told me she thought she was a victim of "Imposter Syndrome."

We discussed a problem one of her development associates had identified: multiple fundraisers were chasing down the same leads and acting at cross-purposes in creating relationships with new donors. The system for keeping those communications straight was practically non-existent, and the associate wanted her leader (my client) to solve the mess.

"I've been working all weekend trying to develop a system everyone will be okay working with," my client said. "And once again, I'm neglecting my family and skipping the 'me-time' I committed to giving myself each weekend."

I asked her why she thought she personally had to do this.

"Because I'm the leader here," she said. "They took a risk hiring me for this position, and I need to prove I can lead."

She was like many leaders I've worked with who

believe they must prove to everyone that they deserve their position day-in and day-out. They think leaders are supposed to know better than everyone else what to do about all the challenging issues that arise. Many leaders feel that they must have all the answers, and worry that if they cannot prove every day that they do, they will be replaced.

I asked my client if she was open to the possibility of asking *her* associate to take some thoughtful time to create a system she thought would fix the problem.

"Oh, I can't do that," she said. "If she comes up with a good system, people will think *she* should have my job! I'm already worried that the board will think I'm an imposter and want to replace me."

We sat with that fear for a while, and I nodded to let her know I understood her anxiety around this issue. I then asked if she was open to a definition of leadership that would give her more freedom and support in her job.

"Of course," she said. "You know I always want to be open."

"Try this on," I said, "like you'd try on a new jacket to see if it fits and feels good. What if it was true that great leaders create leaders, not followers? Great leaders ask for and inspire leadership in others and bring out the best in those people, including those who report to them."

"You mean instead of trying to look like I have all the answers and can do everything myself?" she asked with a self-deprecating smile.

"Yes, exactly. All the best sports coaches and professional athletes surround themselves with great assistants, advisors, trainers, psychologists, nutritionists, fitness gurus and the like, and delegate most of their accountability. The best political and governmental leaders do the same. They surround themselves with experienced people they trust, and empower them to solve things."

My client was intrigued by this idea, and I could tell she wanted to hear more. So, I asked her, "What does the Board want most from you at the end of the day?"

"To raise funds ... to have our group raise as much money as possible."

I said, "And do they really care how that gets done? The details of who does what?"

"No, not really. They just want to see the bottom line of what we've raised in donations continue to grow."

She realized that the Board wasn't overly interested in whether my client was right about things and had all the answers herself. That was only her own personal insecurity, and it had led to a narrow and distorted view of what she, as the leader, should be doing.

The following week she had a meeting with her associate, asked her to articulate the challenge as she saw it, and requested that she give it some thoughtful time and come up with a solution she thought would work. The associate agreed, and the system she created was simple, clear, and functional. My client gave the associate full credit for it. She then requested her team member take on the responsibility of overseeing its execution and managing the lines of accountability.

The fact that great leaders grow leaders all around them is not an original idea of mine that I "teach" to clients. It's an observation. And the great result of being able to talk about this observation in a coaching session with a leader is that it opens up a more effective and generous way to lead people. It also ensures that more thoughtful solutions occur more frequently. Who ultimately deserves credit for that? Whoever is leading the way.

Conclusion

Unbounded Leadership

Command and control-style leaders have been and will continue to be successful, to a point. But the developments and disruptions of the 21st century require that relationships between leadership and team members move well beyond the traditional transaction: "I will pay you for this work to meet your basic needs and provide some benefits (survival). If you do what I say, you can keep getting it (security)."

A team consisting mainly of people only concerned with meeting survival and security needs—and led by leaders who are okay with that—will almost certainly be unable to take an organization where it needs to go. And they will stay put as long as they can.

This is not the case for people who care about and are capable of growing. Unless the organization offers these team members a greater commitment and tangible path for personal development, they will move to organizations where, from their perspectives, they can grow and thrive.

Most organizations accommodated basic needs a long time ago. But the move to fully unlock the door for self-exploration and the development of a higher degree of individual potential has been slow. In leading organizations through the digital, technological, and scientific disruptions pushing humans into higher order "thinking" roles, greater humanity is not just a nicety. It is essential.

In many cultures, religions, and spiritual practices, life is considered a journey toward achieving our highest sense of well-being and wholeness. Although there is no silver bullet definition of "the art of humanity in leadership," leaders supporting their team members in discovering and reaching for their highest potential is a central part of it. This means enabling each individual to feel safe being human in the context of the organization. Being seen not just for their education, skills, and experience, but for their personality, emotions, attitude, fallibility, fears, and the rest of the full complement of attributes that make a human a "whole person."

Being human as a leader means showing up with feeling *and* facilitatating the expression of the full range of civil human dimensions and emotions by the people around them. To show the way, leaders must be willing to pursue greater holistic development themselves and encourage and teach the "way of well-being" within the organization.

Enabling this kind of exploration in an organizational context is not an entirely new idea, but in many instances it is still nascent. It represents a huge opportunity for advancing human development. Better leaders, better team members and better organizations, beget better results.

This may at first seem a bridge too far from *The Leader and The Coach*. But the desire to be recognized for our unique qualities and reach a higher level of potential is precisely what is meant by expressions such as, "A paycheck isn't enough. I am more than my output at work. I need to be seen in my full dimension and possibility." These kinds of statements represent an awareness that humans are integrated beings— indivisible. It doesn't matter where they are or what they are doing. It is and has long been dysfunctional to expect team members (and for that matter, leaders) to check any part of their humanness at the door of the workplace.

We have addressed several ways for leaders to develop a foundation for the transformation that is required, including:

- Creating an environment of psychological safety

- Being more authentic and transparent

- Developing and advancing well-being initiatives

- Creating a sense of belonging and community

- Supporting creativity and collaboration

- Enabling greater autonomy and self-management

- Providing self-development opportunities and recognition

- Enabling and supporting team members in going as far as they can with all that they've got

These practices represent some of the actionable ways to create an environment promoting the integration of individual and leadership development, and to achieve the organization's purpose—the reason for coming together at all.

Effective 21st century leadership requires greater attentiveness and mentoring at the one-to-one level. Steve has provided many anecdotes proving it is no accident that the best coaching is one to one. Human to human. Not title to title, master to apprentice, boss to follower. Listening, learning, and using proven coaching skills and approaches represent ways to open and sustain deeper human connections between leaders and team members.

Unbounded leadership is the continuous process of creating an environment where individuals can discover greater possibility, meaning, and purpose. It is essential for success as we grapple with the myriad requirements for skillful and rapid organizational adaptation and resilience. What, in your leadership status quo, could be more valuable than growing into your highest self and helping others do it too? Doesn't this represent our highest potential as leaders, coaches, and whole human beings?

For more on leadership, and coaching leaders and businesses, subscribe to
The Leader and The Coach blog at:

www.theleaderandthecoach.com

Gratitude

Steve

Heartfelt thanks to my own life and business coach, Steve Hardison. Without his guidance and love, I would not be who or where I am today.

To Kathy, for love and support beyond words.

To Chris Nelson, Brannan Sirratt, Elisa Tidswell, and Carrie Brito for their expert editorial guidance.

And especially to my dear friend Will Keiper, who was the inspiring, driving force behind the content for this book. It was a sheer delight and an honor to be his co-author.

Will

To my coach, muse, and friend Steve Chandler. It was an honor for me to co-create this book with him. He deserves my special thanks for teaching me greater patience and the power of listening and hearing, with my curiosity fully engaged; and

With appreciation for the guidance and truth-telling of our editing professionals, Chris Nelson, Brannan Sirratt, Elisa Tidswell, and Carrie Brito.

Recommended Reading

Fatherhood Is Leadership: Your Playbook for Success, Self-Leadership, and a Richer Life by Devon Bandison

Taking Responsibility: Self-Reliance and the Accountable Life by Nathaniel Branden

Experiments Never Fail: A Guide for the Bored, Unappreciated and Underpaid by Dale Dauten

The Gifted Boss: How to Find, Create and Keep Great Employees by Dale Dauten

The Collaborative Way by Lloyd Fickett

The Ultimate Coach by Amy Hardison and Alan Thompson

The Power of Urgency: Playing to Win with Proactive Urgency by William Keiper

Conscious Capitalism by John Mackey and Raj Sisodia

The Excellence Dividend by Tom Peters

100 Ways to Motivate Others by Scott Richardson and Steve Chandler

Reimagine Teams: The Missing Piece in Team Building to Achieve Breakthrough Results by Mark Samuel

Driving Excellence: How 'The Aggregate System' Turned Microchip Technology from a Failing Company to a Market Leader by Steve Sanghi and Mike J. Jones

Wooden on Leadership by John Wooden

About the Authors

Steve Chandler is the author and co-author of more than 35 books, including the bestsellers *Time Warrior, Reinventing Yourself, 100 Ways to Motivate Yourself,* and *The Prosperous Coach,* among others. He and Will Keiper recently co-authored *The Well-Being Bucket List.*

He has been a seminar leader, sales and leadership trainer, business, leadership, and success coach for more than 30 years. He is the founder and lead teacher in the internationally respected Coaching Prosperity School.

He lives with his family in Birmingham, Michigan, and can be reached through his website at:

www.stevechandler.com

or

www.theleaderandthecoach.com

Will Keiper is a business advisor, leadership coach, and an expert in intensive, short-term, game-changing coaching for businesses. He has been an NYSE, NASDAQ, and private company CEO and board member and is recognized as a pragmatic truth-teller, strategist, and change agent. He is committed to helping humans and businesses desiring transformation to do things differently by seeing things differently.

He is an award-winning nonfiction author, and has written *The Power of Urgency*, *Untethered Aging*, *Life Expectancy – It's Never Too Late to Change Your Game*, and *Cyber Crisis – It's Personal Now*, among others. He and Steve Chandler recently co-authored *The Well-Being Bucket List*. He can be reached at:

www.willkeiper.com

or

www.theleaderandthecoach.com

Made in United States
Orlando, FL
16 September 2022

22482900R00085